Out On The Edge

"A wow of a book—and CD-ROM. Awesome in its depiction of how a church can use electronic and visual media of our time to connect with the unchurched public without dumbing down the message."

William Easum,
author of *Growing Spiritual Redwoods*

"If you and your church want to reach unchurched people with the Good News of Jesus, then this is a must-read book. I felt pumped with excitement as I experienced in print and CD-ROM the ways in which we can reach people who live in the darkness. This book will change the way that you think about worship for the new century."

Dick Wills,
one of the pastors,
Christ Church United Methodist
Fort Lauderdale, Florida

"Communicating Christ to persons who prefer to hear with their eyes and receive truth through relationships and personal experience requires new methods. Slaughter shows us how biblical theology, delivered in new wineskins, transmits life-changing power to people for whom church just doesn't make sense. The step-by-step descriptions for building electronic media into a worship celebration will provide a roadmap for reinventing any congregation's future."

Herb Miller,
publisher of Net Results, and The Parish Paper.

"No pastor I know understands the post-modern, post-literate, and post-Christian world better than Mike Slaughter. More than that, he practices ministry in a congregation that knows how to engage the world for the sake of the gospel. This is a must-read book in a time when fact is out and experience is in. In a culture that is not anti-God but anti-Christian, in lives that are deeply interested in spirituality but not in religious organizations, Mike Slaughter brings us concrete help and direction in worship, small group life, and in self-direct ministry teams. He shares not only what he thinks but what he does."

Tex Sample,
The Robert B. and Kathleen Rogers
professor of church and society,
St. Paul School of Theology.

Out On The Edge

A Wake-Up Call For Church Leaders On The Edge Of The Media Reformation

by Michael Slaughter

Abingdon Press

OUT ON THE EDGE

This book is printed on recycled, acid-free,
elemental-chlorine-free paper

**Library of Congress Cataloging-in-Publication Data
(on file)**

Scripture quotations, unless otherwise indicated, are from *The New
Revised Standard Version* of the Bible, copyright © 1989 by the
National Council of Churches of Christ.

Scripture quotations from *The Message* are noted and used by
permission.

*In Memory of
My Grandparents
Melba and Daniel
Boone Ramage*

CONTENTS

See CD ROM: *Multi-sensory Worship*

Acknowledgments

I am indebted to many people in the creation of this project. The people of Ginghamsburg Church have been the faithful model that encourages me to risk forward in my journey with Jesus. It has been an honor to serve such a people at such a strategic point in time.

I am indebted to staff colleagues and good friends who have helped me work out the ministry models found within this project. These include Mike Lyons, Kim Miller, Jeff Friend, Ray Jones, Len Wilson, Tom Tumblin, Tammy Kelley and John Jung. Debra Welder has worked with me for three years as an administrative assistant. I am grateful for her contributions in research and word processing as this project matured.

Certainly I must mention the persons that I meet with every Thursday morning who ask me the hard questions and give me wise counsel: Vic Haddad, Mike Cargill, John Ward and Dennis Mikel. I am thankful for young friends, such as Casey Wead, who encourage us to attempt great things for God.

Finally, I am thankful for Carolyn White Slaughter, who is my best friend and traveling companion for more than a quarter of a century—and who provided the gift of our children, Kristen and Jonathan.

FOREWORD

How many open country churches average more than three thousand in worship every weekend? How many mainline Protestant congregations have three times as many people worshiping God every weekend as they have members? How many congregations are using the electronic visual media to proclaim the Gospel of Jesus Christ?

These are three of the story lines in this remarkable book about one of the most exciting new forms of ministry on the North American continent. If you want to visit a tested working model of the worshiping community of the twenty-first century, spend a long weekend with this congregation that meets in a building on a county road out in the country a dozen miles north of Dayton, Ohio. If you cannot do that, read this book and study the CD-ROM disk about multi-sensory worship that is included.

This book also illustrates a half dozen of the distinctive characteristics of the best churches of today and tomorrow. First, and from this observer's perspective, the most distinctive, when the laity are challenged to be engaged in doing ministry, they respond with enthusiasm, commitment, and effectiveness, *if the challenge is to meaningful ministry, if the institutional environment is supportive of their involvement, if the appropriate training is provided, and if the assignment matches the passion, gifts, and skills of the volunteer.*

Second, the large regional church can reach and serve a mixture of people, including those who reside in a large central city, in the newer suburbs, in the small town, and out in the open country. The call to mission has replaced geographical proximity as the defining characteristic of the people to be served.

Third, *Out on the Edge* is evidence that a growing number of congregations welcome everyone who is interested to come and worship God with us, but have a high threshold for anyone who seeks to become a member. Participation is wide open, but unreserved commitment is the synonym for membership.

Fourth, *Out on the Edge* is an outstanding example of how lives are transformed as people move from passive believers to active disciples.

Fifth, *Out on the Edge* is an outstanding example of how staff-volunteer teams are replacing the old configuration in which each program staff member worked alone with his or her committee. The old staff formula was based on the hope that one plus one plus one plus one plus one equals five. The new configuration is based on the assumption that three plus five plus seven equals sixty in terms of creativity, productivity, innovation, and middle-sized miracles.

Finally, *Out on the Edge* illustrates very clearly that the road to a new tomorrow is paved with patience, persistence, passion, trust, creativity, patience, tenacity, zeal, determination, innovation, persistence, openness, diligence, passion, commitment, patience, outreach, passion, persistence, endurance, disappointments, passion, excitement, generosity, trust, creativity, outreach, patience, and enthusiasm. Passion, patience, and persistence are key ingredients on that road to transformation.

Lyle E. Schaller, Parish Consultant
Author of *The Church Consultant* on CD-ROM

"Church Just Doesn't Make Sense"

It's the first hot, humid day of spring and the air conditioner isn't working! Carolyn calls Art from the local heating and cooling company. Art's father started the business in our town of sixty five hundred in the 1950's. As in many small towns our size, you get to know and give your business to local folk. We've called Art's dad and now Art for the eighteen years that we have lived in Tipp City.

I stroll over to the side of the house where Art is working on the unit.

> "Hi, Art. Does it look like it's low on freon?"
> "No, I checked the freon. It looks like it's a compressor problem. How long have you had the unit?"
> "Well . . . we built this house four years ago."

> "You're in luck—it has a five-year warranty. You'll only have to pay the price of installation. I'll send Jim out to do the installation as soon as the unit comes in. You know Jim. He goes to your church."

Well, I am not sure if I know Jim or not. Many "Jims" are part of the ministry of Ginghamsburg Church. But this is a real opportunity to ask Art about his own faith background.

> "Art, do you go to church anywhere?"
> "No, not me. My wife goes to the Lutheran Church, with the kids . . . where we were married. I'm like my dad. The women go to church and the men stay home and get things done."
> "Do you believe in God?" I ask Art.
> "Oh yeah . . . I believe in God. I was even born again once! If I want to meet with God, I just go out into the woods or fishing . . . or some place beautiful.
> Church just doesn't make sense."

The dictionary defines *sense* as the ability to receive stimuli through any of the five senses (sight, hearing, touch, smell and taste) including the sixth sense. To make sense means to be understandable.

Most People Cannot Make Sense of Church

The way we are "doing church" in North America is not effectively bringing the Good News to the majority of God's creation. Statistics are one way to verify this assertion. Every other year George Gallup traces the percentage of the US population that attends church on a regular basis (at least once monthly). The results have held fairly constant at 42-44 percent for the past 40 years, though dipped to 38 percent in 1997.

George Barna, who does an annual survey using polling data to get at the percentage of the U.S. population that have attended church at least once in the last six months, reports a significant downward slide. His findings show that from 1994—1996, those who reported attending church dropped from 42 percent to 38 percent.

Many sociologists are not as generous with their findings. They believe church attendance figures reported by pollsters have been exaggerated. A study published in 1994 by the University of Notre Dame found that the national average was a mere 26.7 percent.[i] In 1993, one study concluded that only 19.6 percent of Protestants and 28 percent of Catholics were in church on any given week.[ii] Church attendance in Canada is estimated at 14 to 17 percent and in some provinces as low as 4 to 7 percent.[iii] My own denomination estimates the 1996 membership loss at 42,000. That is an improvement over the 49,308 loss posted in 1995 and the 62,267 members lost in 1994.[iv]

Gallup and Barna studies are based on how a person says she or he behave and not on direct observation. If you ask a person if he votes, he will say what he would like to be true about his citizenship and not how he actually behaves. The same behavior is at play with religion. Approximately 40 percent of persons say they are in church at least once a month. Religious sociologists C. Kirk Hadaway (United Church of Christ) and Penny Marler (Southern Baptist) went to four representative counties around the USA and identified every house of worship and then counted heads. They assert that only 22 percent of Protestants and 26 percent of Roman Catholics in the USA are in church at least once a month.

Church attendance is heading in a downward spiral at an accelerating pace, while personal interest in spirituality is growing. Art, the repairman, speaks for the masses: "Church just doesn't make sense!" It's not that individuals don't believe in God. The same polls show that overwhelmingly American people report belief in God, but they don't expect to find God in church.

Many causes for this decline have been proposed (see *Church and Denominational Growth,* edited by C. Kirk Hadaway and David Roozen, Abingdon Press, 1993). Church attendance in North America is in accelerating decline. Most churches are not speaking a language that makes sense to a culture asking spiritual questions.

When "God Movements" Happen

It had been only fifty days since the revolutionary event of the first Easter morning. A small group of Jesus' followers (120) had been meeting in an upstairs rental space for the purpose of prayer, mutual encouragement, and the promise of empowerment that would come through God's Spirit. They had seen Jesus with their own eyes, heard his words, touched his wounds. Jesus had come from the grave. This reversal in human history became the key evidence of God's ultimate reality and ultimate love. God would empower this small church to take the message of Jesus and the resurrection to the whole world.

Don't miss this miracle! God empowers small churches to speak the language of ultimate reality and ultimate love to unchurched people all around us. That is what the miracle of Pentecost is about.

> "When the Feast of Pentecost came, they were all
> together in one place. Without warning there was a
> sound like a strong wind, gale force—no one could tell
> where it came from. It filled the whole building. Then,
> like a wildfire, the Holy Spirit spread through their
> ranks, and they started speaking in a number of different
> languages as the Spirit prompted them.

There were many Jews staying in Jerusalem just then, devout pilgrims from all over the world. When they heard the sound, they came on the run. Then when they heard, one after another, their own mother tongues being spoken, they were thunderstruck. They couldn't for the life of them figure out what was going on, and kept saying, "Aren't these all Galileans? How come we're hearing them talk in our various mother tongues?

. . . They're speaking our languages, describing God's mighty works!"

Acts 2:1-11, *The Message* (emphasis added)

An Overview of the Edge

This work addresses a strategy for ministry that bridges the twenty-first century Church with our predominantly unchurched culture.

The book is divided into three parts. Part One deals with the Media Reformation as a life or death issue for the Church.

Chapter 1 begins this discussion with an examination of the current North American culture. We live in a post-modern, post-Christian, post-literate age. My premise is that the time in which we live is much like the pre-Christian culture of the Book of Acts. There is a new fullness of time for the Gospel of Jesus Christ. In chapter 2 I discuss the whole purpose of incarnational-cultural ministry. Jesus had a market-place theology. In chapter 3 I show the shape of radical new wineskins. I examine why churched persons resist change, and why change management occurs prior to adapting new cultural practices to reach tomorrow's generations. We look at four communication-technology shifts that have taken place during the life of the Church, with emphasis on electronic media.

In Part Two we move into the development of a practical strategy for transformation; a strategy that moves beyond the abstract, cerebral model of the literate age. I present a model that is more experiential—a journey to wellness and purpose. Chapter 4 deals with the first part of this journey: Involving people in the experience of Celebration (worship) that makes sense in our current life context. We talk about the importance of worship and address the critical issue of designing worship for a post-literate culture. I advocate the design and development of worship as a multi-sensory experience.

Chapter 5 introduces the importance of Cell (a small group of intimate friends) as the second critical strategic factor in the process of transformation. Persons are changed as they live their lives in small support groups. Notice the success of TV programming that is built around this theme. *Seinfeld* and *Friends* are two examples of small groups of "friends" who are traveling the journey together, and testing their ideas and values on each other. Chapter 6 deals with the final piece of the strategic plan: helping people to get in touch with God's Call (relevant mission). My premise is that people are transformed as we involve them in the life-rhythm of Celebration, Cell and Call.

Part Three examines team building; how to build high-powered teams that will speak effectively to the present culture. Multimedia is labor intensive. We cannot do ministry in the twenty-first century as we have done it in the past. We must build teams of high-powered specialists. Most of these church staff will not come from the seminaries. Chapter 7 exposes mindsets that must change to build effective team ministry. A staff group or committee is not necessarily a team and does not exist merely because you name it a "team." Chapter 8 is called "Multi-sensory Worship." It is a CD-ROM, offering a multi-media experience that allows you to follow a Celebration team in their experience of worship design from Wednesday through Sunday. This book proposes that any congregation can, and every viable congregation eventually will, form celebration experiences based in relevant and emerging types of multi-sensory ministry.

Part One

Why The Media Reformation Is A Life Or Death Issue

"This year, 9000 Protestant churches will close across the United States. Most will close because they couldn't compete; closing was a more attractive alternative than thinking."

Lyle E. Schaller[v]

Introduction:
The Electronic Media
Pentecost

99.9 percent of Americans have televisions;
97 percent have plumbing.[vi]

I phoned home from a conference about the Media Reformation. During the course of the conversation, Jonathan, my fifteen year old son and sports enthusiast, informed me that Rick Pitino would probably be leaving the head coaching position at the University of Kentucky. He had been offered seventy million dollars to return to coaching in the NBA. This was a devastating blow for the UK fans, since Pitino had restored Kentucky to the epitome of national basketball prominence in his eight-season stint.

"Where did you read this, Jonathan?"

"I didn't read it. I *saw* it on ESPN Sports Center."

See not *read* is the word for this generation. This is the generation that has been saturated with media from the day they were born. From the Brady Bunch to MTV. From McDonalds' Golden Arches to Nike. This generation, often referred to as Busters or Generation X, has been raised on an electronic playground. Atari, Nintendo, and Sega have been their baby-sitters; *Sesame Street* and *MTV* their tutors. In a typical week 38 percent of Busters watch *MTV*.[vii] Bill Clinton knew the importance of this communication medium when he appeared on *MTV* during the 1992 presidential campaign. It is the most widely viewed channel among Busters.

Our children view more than 5000 hours of television by age five.[viii] At age seven, if she's anything like the typical kid, she will watch some 20,000 TV commercials a year.[ix] This saturation in multi-sensory images is what we mean by the impact of media on values and beliefs. My kids would point to the Golden Arches of McDonalds through the car windows before they had a fifty-word vocabulary. For years it was the only place they lobbied to eat during vacation trips.

Our children are not the only persons raised in an audio-visual culture. From *I Love Lucy, Howdy Doody, The Wonderful World of Disney, Leave It To Beaver, Gunsmoke, Father Knows Best, The Twilight Zone, Ed Sullivan, Dallas,* countless hours of soap operas, *Saturday Night Live, Oprah, Phil, Jerry, Geraldo* to *ER* —TV has defined our values, styles, vocabulary, and choices. Two generations have grown up in a mass-media culture. TV is the defining medium. Now we bring on the Internet, where the values, lifestyles, and new vocabularies are piped on to personal television or computer screens without regulators or censors.

Personal focus on the screen has created a radical paradigm shift in the way "things make sense" to children, youth, and adults. A recent national study tried to determine the impact TV has had on the way college students learn.

- They expect to be entertained. Serious topics and serious discussions are viewed as boring.
- They are visually oriented. They relate more quickly to pictures than to words.
- They are not attentive to lecture-format presentations, which often lack motion, color, rapid changes, sound effects, visual effects, music, and drama.
- They become bored easily, unless information is fragmented and packaged according to the TV formula.
- They dislike history. TV does not deal with the historical facts effectively, nor does the TV generation.
- They dislike reading. Reading demands concentration and imagination. The reader must construct the scenes, sets, and characters. Reading is hard work, compared to watching TV.[x]

No wonder the Church isn't making sense for most people in the North American culture. We are speaking a different language. We are still using the language of a literate culture in a post-literate visual age.

The Old and The New

The Protestant Reformation was a movement of God's Spirit that rode the wave of the latest technology: the printing press. Printing was invented in Europe by Johannes Gutenberg between 1440 and 1456. Printing ushered in the age of literacy. Martin Luther seized the medium and in so doing "spoke the language of the culture". His translation of the Bible into the common language of the people (German) was mass-produced in an inexpensive form. At first this new medium was perceived with much skepticism and disdain by the official Church. But as the Reformation grew, a few Catholic cardinals realized the advantage of making the message of the Church readily available in a means that "made sense" to the person on the street. The Church began to develop and print catechisms and pamphlets that fueled the flames of the Counter-Reformation.

The sixteenth and seventeenth centuries became a new time of Pentecost. A movement of God's Spirit occurred because the Church was poised to adapt a new cultural technology. *Pilgrim's Progress,* numbered among the great literary works, was written in 1675 by John Bunyan. He wrote for the purpose of sharing Jesus Christ with the unchurched. The impact of this work far exceeded his wildest expectations.

Electronic media is to the "Reformation" of the twenty-first century what Gutenberg's press was to the Reformation of the sixteenth and seventeenth centuries. TV, having come of age in the 1950s, has changed the way we learn and our perceptions of what makes sense. The effective congregation of the twenty-first century will be part of the Church that makes use of multimedia. The New Reformation will speak the language of the culture and employ the communication technology that shapes the culture.

It might seem too strong to say that there is no alternative for the viability of the future Church, but I mean to be even more bold in claiming that the Media Reformation is a life or death issue for the Church.

Chapter 1

A Post-literate Age

"Nobody I know reads reviews.
The printed word is going the way
of the dinosaur."
Bruce Willis

G reat leaders have always been able to "read" the times and speak the language of the culture. God doesn't act in a vacuum. God acts in specific times, cultures and places.

> "But when the fullness of time had come, God sent his Son, born of a woman, born under the law, in order to redeem those who were under the law, so that we might receive adoption as children."
>
> Galatians 4:4

Why was Jesus born in a particular time, in a specific culture and place? When the time was right . . . full . . . pregnant with infinite possibilities . . . God acted. Jesus put it in these words:

"The time is right, and God's kingdom has come near; repent and believe in God's good news!"

The early church was born in an era of providential preparation. The political, social and spiritual climate was ripe for the message of God's good news. The Roman government ruled the largest part of the known world, having wrestled control from Hellenistic Greece. Rome imposed through its rule a global mindset, relative peace, a universal language (Koine Greek) and a massive highway system. All of these factors together contributed to free movement throughout the Empire. A world information highway, as it were. This pre-Christian culture was the right time for the Church to take the radical message of the Gospel to the ends of the earth. God's people maximized the moment. They spoke the language of the Gospel in a sensible fashion to the diverse cultures that made up the Roman Empire.

> "While Peter was still speaking, the Holy Spirit fell upon all who heard the word. The circumcised believers who had come with Peter were astounded that the gift of the Holy Spirit had been poured out even on the Gentiles"
>
> Acts 10:44-45.

Even the Gentiles heard the message in their own cultural context. Why? Because the leaders of the Church understood the times and were intentional about being students of the culture. The apostle Paul put it this way:

> To the Jews I became as a Jew, in order to win Jews. To those under the law I became as one under the law (though I myself am not under the law) so that I might win those under the law.
> To those outside the law *(pagans in Paul's mind)* I became as one outside the law (though I am not free from God's law but am under Christ's law) so that I might win those outside the law. *I have become all things to all people, that I might by all means save some."*
>
> 1 Corinthians 9:20-22

Paul was raised in a rigid, exclusive, monotheistic culture, which we now refer to as early Judaism. He learned a religious language with all of the buzzwords known only by the people within the culture. As a result of an encounter with Christ, this religious leader was willing to change paradigms and become a student again. He was committed to learn new models of communication. Why? "I do it all for the sake of the Gospel, so that I may share in its blessings" (1 Corinthians 9:23).

Throughout Scripture, leaders are portrayed with an understanding of the age in which they live and communicate. This is true of prophets who served as advisors or antagonists to kings and queens. It is true of Moses, the first leader of God's people. "So Moses was instructed in all the wisdom of the Egyptians and was powerful in his words and deeds" (Acts 7:22).

Why did God choose Moses to be an effective wilderness leader? Moses was a student of the dominant culture of his time and place. From birth, as an adopted child, he was immersed in all the wisdom of the Egyptians. By the grace of God, Moses was not contaminated with the content, but he was able to speak God's prophetic truth in the language of Pharaoh. For the next forty years, Moses would communicate the truth of the God of Abraham, Isaac, and Jacob to a people who had become mesmerized and immersed in the polytheism of Egypt.

Moses remained God's leader throughout the instability of a wilderness sojourn, on the way to a promising future. The Church, as we know it, is also in a wilderness. God's people are asking for wilderness leaders: women and men who thoroughly understand the culture and can speak God's prophetic truth to the generations of the twenty-first century.

A Hinge Point In History

We live in a post-modern, post-Christian, post-literate world. The prefix "post" means *after*. The timing of our human experience comes after the age of modernity, Christendom, and literacy but it is not yet something else. Post-modernity is an in-between time; a "not yet" time, or a hinge point in history. We stand between two different periods in God's creative purposes. Modernity is over, but we don't know what is coming next. It's frightening, but what an incredible time to be alive! We are privileged to be part of Christ's transforming force in shaping the future.

Many definitions are floating around for "post-modern" culture. So many meanings are proposed that the term itself is a kind of self-fulfilling prophecy. Here's one that "works" for me: *post-modern* means *post-scientific*. I do not mean the rejection of the scientific method, but the rejection of the premise that all truth can be defined only by science, by the five empirical senses. Modernity is a term that goes by other labels: the Age of Enlightenment or the Age of Reason. The basic premise of modernity is that all truth has its basis in matter and can be determined or measured by the scientific method, which uses the five senses (taste, touch, smell, hearing, and sight) to test hypotheses about causes and effects. If an idea or hypothesis can't be proven by science, then it is not "true." People of the pre-modern times, who lived with a world view of faith, are considered by Modernists as superstitious, primitive, or easily persuaded by magical thinking. The focus on theology as the Queen of the Sciences was shifted to biology, zoology, psychology, and physics. The center of authority was no longer the omnipotent God but the autonomous human being. Immanuel Kant epitomized the age of modernity in the famous phrase "dare to know".[xi]

Post-modernity rejects the rigid, narrow idea that all truth can be known or measured solely by the scientific method. Life is too complex to limit our understanding of the cosmos strictly to matter alone. There seems to be an inherent spiritual quality woven into the fabric of creation and sounded in the rhythms of life. Post-modernity is a reaction against the rationalistic philosophy of modernity, which has failed to meet spiritual needs. For the post-modern, fact is out—feeling is in! Howard Snyder wrote about this trend in 1975:

"The situation today looks like a replay of the first century. Both a contemporary conservative Protestant (Francis Schaeffer) and a secular political scientist (Zbignieve Brzezinski) have spoken of man's escape from reason. Experiencing is the thing, whether through political radicalism, drugs, communal living, glossolalia or oriental mysticism; one has only to look at the mess we are in today, it is said, to see where rationalism leads. A return to romanticism has set in."[xii]

Many people of Jesus' time rejected the tired and wearisome Greek forms of rationalism, idealism, and philosophy. They were seeking meaning in the many different varieties of Roman mystery religions. The fullness of time was birthed in an atmosphere of spiritual quest and hunger. Stoicism and Epicureanism grew into selfish individualism, and thus some persons began to seek a more spiritual approach to life. Does this search sound familiar? North America is in the middle of a "god rush." There is evidence of a spiritual awakening, even in Hollywood. Who would have thought that a television program called "Touched By An Angel" would be close to the top of the ratings? Look at the proliferation of books on the supernatural. Check out the titles that deal with angels. John Travolta plays a macho but crude angel in the movie *Michael. Angels in the Outfield* probes our cultural myths about baseball and fatherhood. Our culture is open to and, in many cases, pursuing the supernatural. The "X-Files" phenomena, the "Psychic Friends Network," attempt to put us in touch with extra-terrestrials. Is there life on Mars? *Life Magazine* reports that "Astrology is hotter than it's been in four centuries."[xiii] Americans believe almost anything—as long as it is not in the Bible.

Post-modern means to be open to mystery and to regard the supernatural as plausible. What better time to be alive to the Gospel! We have an opportunity to present the Gospel to a culture which is open to truth that is not validated by science! In terms of communication, our mission field is very much like the culture of the first-century Church. Our anticipated audience is seeking a more spiritual approach to life, even in the workplace, which has long been segregated by secularizing forces.

While still very new, the trend is starting to go beyond fringe companies or vaguely foreign institutions like the World Bank. Lotus Development Corp. has a "Soul Committee" that makes sure the company lives up to its stated values. Boeing recruited poet David Whyte to read poems and regale top managers with fables as part of a program to revitalize their spirits on the job.[xiv]

Sometimes companies borrow religious terms as a hook for employees. For example, Microsoft refers to its publicist as the Director of Evangelism.

A god rush can be a lot like a gold rush. With any gold rush, there is a whole lot of fool's gold. Fool's gold and foolish gods. The Church, however, has a tremendous window of opportunity to share the good news of God's Son with a world that is seeking spiritual solutions rather than the pseudo or cynical veneer of religious jargon.

Post-christian

"While Peter and John were speaking to the people, the priests, the captain of the temple and the Sadducees came to them, much annoyed because they were teaching the people and proclaiming that in Jesus there is the resurrection of the dead . . . So they called them and ordered them not to speak or teach at all in the name of Jesus."

Acts 4:1-2; 18

Spirituality is in. Specific claims about spirituality are out. North American culture is not anti-God. It is anti-Christian. Christianity has always been perceived as a threat to the predominant culture because Christianity is presupposed as an intolerant or exclusive perspective.

The Bible makes claims that "There is salvation in no one else, for there is no other name under heaven given among mortals by which we must be saved" (Acts 4:12). Or the Gospel of John recalls this saying of Jesus: "I am the way, and the truth and the life. No one comes to the Father except through me" (John 14:6). These claims are extremely controversial outside the walls of the Church, and sometimes problematic within.

It is costly to follow Jesus. Peter and John discovered the cost and controversy when they were taking the message of Jesus and the resurrection to the streets. Their persistence resulted in their arrest and a night in jail. The crime was not "spirituality" or belief in God. The Roman culture had a deep tolerance for spirituality but a deadly intolerance for specific claims that threatened its domination.

When it comes to truth, the post-Christian culture is very much like the pre-Christian culture of the Roman Empire. Even as the culture rejects science as the arbiter of truth, it rejects Christianity (or any form of organized religion) as the standard-bearer for truth. Billions of persons on our planet are comfortable with the concept of "many gods" or "many truths" and are uneasy with those who emphasize absolute truth before invoking tolerance. The rejection of science as the arbiter of truth is, for such persons, inseparable from the resignation that all human experience is relative or ambiguous.

Supreme Court Justice Antonin Scalia, a Roman Catholic, spoke at a college prayer breakfast. He spoke of personal cost: "We are fools for Christ's sake. We must pray for courage to endure the scorn of the sophisticated world." His remarks drew fire from Barry Lynn of Americans United for Separation of Church and State. "This clearly undermines public confidence in his objectivity regarding religious controversies," Lynn said.[xv]

Spirituality is in. Specific claims about Jesus are out. So when I attempt to persuade you that cultural relevance is a life and death matter, be forwarned that the Gospel is hard and offensive to many. Effective communication is not about compromise. A compelling Gospel must be clear about the truth in the language of the culture.

The post-Christian culture is a culture of "many gods" that rejects absolutes. This generation is the first generation that has been raised totally outside of the Church. Our culture is not agnostic. It is "ignostic" (a term George Hunter coined in *How to Reach Secular People*, Nashville: Abingdon Press, 1992). They are ignorant when it comes to recognition of biblical ideas and Christian language. People do not understand basic concepts that we take for granted. For example, our worship team was doing a series on the theme "grace." We sent our media team downtown during the lunch hour. We simply asked the question "What is grace?" Most people didn't have a clue.

See CD ROM: *Multi-sensory Worship*

"What is Grace?"

The people with whom we are communicating the good news of Jesus Christ are very much like the pre-Christian people of the first century. They do not understand our book, our language, our beliefs, or the behaviors that we expect of one another. Persuasive communication requires listening to the presenting needs of other persons. We must learn their language, define or understand their actual needs, and communicate the life-saving truth of God's love.

Post-literate

For centuries Christians have been called "People of The Book." Our faith journey is built around the study and application of biblical principles. Martin Luther's *Sola Scriptura* (only Scripture) approach to the faith fanned the flames of the Reformation. Luther's translation of the Bible into the common language of the people capitalized on the new age of literacy. The new technological means of printing put the Bible into the hands of the masses. John Wesley, 200 years later, was a beneficiary of Luther's biblical literacy reformation. "My ground is the Bible. Yea, I am a Bible-bigot. I follow it in all things, both great and small."[xvi]

How can we be "People of The Book" in a world where 50 percent are illiterate, 20 percent struggle with literacy and the remaining 30 percent of us receive most of our information from some other source than the printed text? A professor of communication reported to me that the average college graduate reads less than two books per year.

The open Bible on the altar of the congregation has been an important image for the human discovery of truth. Television and computer monitors (which are really television screens) pose a severe challenge to the symbol. The generation born after 1960 has been raised in a culture that is visually dominated. This generation places a far greater emphasis on sight, sound, and sensations. My generation would buy 45s, get together with a group of friends and *listen* to the latest songs by the Beatles, Stones, Bob Dylan or the Supremes. This generation has been raised in an MTV culture that has brought sight and sound together. They *watch* Jakob Dylan on music videos. Lyle Schaller asks the right question. "Where will (this) generation go to church? How will the new reformation speak to this generation?"[xvii]

Post-literate means we can no longer afford to pursue our ministry in the old, tired, linear, literate way. The sight and sound generation calls for a multi-sensory experience. Post-literate means that 100 percent of us get *most* of our information from some other source than the printed text!

Why Marketing?

If the Church is willing to address the presenting needs of the twenty-first century culture, we then become students of marketing. Marketing, however, is disdained with skepticism by much of the Church. It is deemed as a psychological threat to the authority which was conveyed to many of us by the "laying on of hands" when we became church leaders. "Those who use marketing tactics must be "selling out or pandering to irreligious wants and desires." When fighting with marketing as a tactic for understanding those who are outside our walls, we tend to react to the abuses of marketing, which are a manipulation of our vices: Joe Camel idealizes smoking for adolescents, or Calvin Klein features sexualized children who are barely out of puberty.

We don't stop seeking growth as disciples, however, because of the TV evangelist scandals of the 1980s, the growing divorce rate among clergy, or the racist, sexist views that still exist among those in authority in much of the Church. We don't run from the Church just because we perceive hypocrisy. We attempt to differentiate the bad practice from good; we strive to practice the more healthy way when listening to the other.

Marketing is a means for learning to identify felt needs. Marketing is the practice of finding solutions that meet felt needs and effectively communicating those solutions to persons who perceive the needs. The solution may offer a benefit to the other, which is entirely unexpected, more costly, and ultimately transforming. But a marketing orientation to ministry presumes that the people of God cannot surprise or exceed the expectations of those who are not yet part of God's people, unless we understand their needs in the language that they speak.

Women and men in the post-modern culture are tired. Many work more than one job. They are emotionally and spiritually depleted, which is why they seek for something better. The only communication that will connect with their fatigue and yearning is communication that speaks to relevant life issues. Effective marketing in the church involves:

1. Listening;
2. Identifying felt needs and relevant life issues;
3. Developing a strategy to bridge God's solution to felt needs;
4. Effectively communicating the solution.

Cultural Felt Needs

Nike is a master at reading the felt needs of post-moderns. The Nike advertisements never mention athletic wear. From Tiger Woods, to women who are making their way onto the basketball court, Nike gives a thirty-second experience. At the end of the commercial you *feel* something. "Wow!" I find myself saying to others in the room. "Did you see that?" Nike suggests that their products offer an experience! Experience is the primary need of the generations that will live well into the twenty-first century. People are not coming to our churches because they don't believe in God. Pollsters tell us that most of North America reports belief in God and more than half believe that Jesus Christ was the Son of God. People aren't coming to our churches because all they expect to hear is information and reasoned correction. Post-moderns are not looking for information *about* God. We are suffering from an information overload, which creates a muggy and clammy feeling that we have "been there, done that." This saturation of information contributes to the sense of ambiguity about Christian truth. This generation is looking for an experience of God, and they don't expect to find God in church.

An understanding of this basic principle of "felt need" would guide a worship team (which we prefer to label as the "celebration team") in the design of the annual Easter celebration. The celebration team knows that post-moderns are not looking for evidence. How can you explain the miracle of the resurrection? You can't! You can only experience its power in everyday living. Post-moderns understand mystery and living out of a sense of the unexplainable. Notice the success of the TV hit series *The X Files*. A celebration team would build the worship experience around an *X Files* theme by calling it "The Easter Files." The emphasis would

See CD ROM: *Multi-sensory Worship*

"Easter Files"

be on living out of the unexplainable. The team could design advertising (radio, TV, Internet, and newspaper) around this theme.

At Ginghamsburg, we were not surprised when 4,994 showed up for this celebration of God's ultimate sacrifice. By linking the mystery of the cross to unexplainable experiences elsewhere in our culture, we measured an increase of 1,500 more persons who heard startling news, when compared to the previous year. God's solution was bridged to a personal felt need, which we define as the desire to live out of the unexplainable. To rediscover the awe and wonder of life, faith and mystery.

Generational Felt Needs

The "twentysomething" generation is absent from nearly all our churches. This generation is not even finding its way readily into the rapidly growing mega-churches. How can marketing principles help us identify the felt needs of this group?

We got serious about asking these questions about Generation X in 1995. Prior to this time we assumed that the same contemporary worship style that was effective in reaching the unchurched Boomer would also be effective in reaching the Buster. Wrong assumption! The children of Boomers have very different felt needs. We worked the process.

1. Listened (research, study, surveys, visited three churches that were effectively speaking to the felt needs of the unchurched Buster);
2. Identified felt needs and relevant life issues;
3. Developed a strategy;
4. Communicated the solution to people experiencing felt need.

See CD ROM: *Multi-sensory Worship*

A proven strategy is to bring a Generation X staff person who would build a team to do "Gen X" worship. For example, Ray Jones came on staff in January of 1996 and started Souljourn, a Gen X worship experience in January of 1997. Attendance averages approximately 300 after six months with Stage 2 Bible studies offered after the worship experience. Bridging God's truth and healing with people's felt needs is what Jesus's incarnation is all about. The incarnation is the act of God who meets people right where they live. You and I live in a post-modern, post-Christian, post-literate world that is searching for the unexplainable, awe-inspiring mystery that can only be satisfied by an incarnate God who comes in the Christ.

Chapter 2

The Word Became Flesh!

"The word became flesh and blood and moved into the neighborhood. We saw the glory with our own eyes"
John 1:14, *The Message*

*"What if God was one of us?
Just a slob like one of us?"*
Joan Osbourne, Pop Music Artist

How can you grasp an infinite God? How can I even begin to understand? Wait a minute? What did you say? The word ... the unspoken thought ... the mind of God ... became visible ... and moved to live in the neighborhood?

That's right ... God became flesh and blood ... brought it down on the asphalt, to where the rubber meets the road. God meets needs that even a preschooler can grasp! "Jesus loves me, this I know." God lets me and you experience the glory of God on a multi-sensory level.

> "We declare to you what was from the beginning,
> what we have seen with our own eyes, what we have
> looked at and touched with our hands, concerning the
> word of life."
>
> 1 John 1:1

God is a communicating God. Jesus is passionate about letting the whole world know about God's relentless, untiring love. God is a God who is in Pursuit. God pursues the tired and the weary, the widow and the orphan, the hurting and the oppressed, the up and over, the down and out, the heterosexual and the homosexual.

God's love bottoms out in the "99 and 1" principle. You know the story. People with leprosy and all kinds of other ugly conditions are coming to listen to Jesus. Outcasts are offensive to religious people who use their faith as a shield against sickness and poverty. "This fellow welcomes sinners and eats with them." So Jesus told them the story.

> "Which one of you, having a hundred sheep and los-
> ing one of them, does not leave the ninety nine in the
> wilderness and go after the one that is lost until he finds
> it? And when he has found it, he lays it on his shoulders,
> shouts for joy and carries it home."

Can you imagine how Jesus does for the sheep what it cannot do for itself? He picks it up and carries it home! When he gets home he calls his friends and neighbors, and they party hearty! "I tell you the truth, there will be more joy in heaven over one sinner who repents than over ninety-nine people who are already in the house" (Luke 15:1-7).

If God is in hot pursuit, then the agenda of the church is the one— not the 99 who are safe and cozy!

A Market-place Theology

Call it what it is: street theology. It isn't the kind of righteous religious talk that is popular in the synagogue or temple. Jesus is rather . . . crude. Yes, that's how I'd put it. Jesus is rather crude, and even rude at times. He uses common metaphors: "Salt is good; but if salt loses its taste, how can its saltiness be restored? It is fit neither for the soil nor the manure pile . . . "(Luke 14:34-35). Flavorless salt can't cover up the smell of one's manure. Was I too crude? No apology from me. Jesus definitely had a street theology. It startled the people in the streets. They turned out in droves to hear him speak. They thought he was more interesting than scribes (editors) and lawyers (conference delegates). Jesus had a greater sense of authenticity, a fleshly power which could "make sense" of human needs and cut through the theological jargon or rationalization.

> "You have heard that it was said, 'you shall not commit adultery.' But I say to you that everyone who looks at a woman with lust has already committed adultery with her in his heart. If your right eye causes you to sin, tear it out and throw it away; it is better for you to lose one of your members than for your whole body to be thrown into hell."
>
> Matthew 5:27-29

The theology of Jesus seemed to take root among the ordinary people, the people who understood the street. It didn't play very well in the temple. It seems that Jesus was never able to accomplish much with the people in the temple. He made an important declaration and read some Scripture. But he met more resistance than hospitality. Perhaps that is why most of Jesus' miraculous healings and transformations happened out in the streets. Did not Paul the religious prosecutor encounter the risen Christ on the Damascus Road?

On the very first Easter day the risen Christ could not be found in a temple or church. He was out walking on the Emmaus Road, out walking with two of his disciples who did not yet recognize him. But their eyes would be opened. The Ethiopian had a life-transforming encounter with Jesus on the Gaza Road. Blind Bartemaeus experienced Jesus' healing touch right on the berm of the Jericho Road.

Jesus had a market-place theology. He met people where they lived. He walked where they walked. While out in the streets, his message didn't play very well in the temple or the academy.

Worship in the Temple

I have been on a church staff in some capacity since 1972. Controversy is constant. There is always some underlying power struggle over the visible direction of the church. Different factions within the church bicker over strongly held points of view. One group urges that "The church needs to be quiet and reflective. We've gotten too contemporary around this place!" And another group feels that "We need more praise and worship. We don't sing as much as we used to!" "The music is too loud" or "the music is not loud enough." "Why do we perform drama in the church?" "The church worship experience needs to be very sensitive to the seeker." "Why do we have a media screen in church. We get enough TV at home!"

Worship that communicates to persons on the street will produce a throbbing, constant underbelly of tension in the temple. Thirty of the original ninety people who attended worship left during the first two years of my current pastorate. Over 200 people left the church when we began using the new wineskin of multi-sensory media. Many of those reasoned that we had in some way compromised the integrity of the Gospel.

Leadership of reformation is never easy. You open yourself to misunderstanding. Jesus was misunderstood even by his own disciples. "This teaching is difficult; who can accept it? .·. . Because of this many of his disciples turned back and no longer went about with him" (John 6:60, 66).

Some people have very explicit and different ideas about the purpose of the Church; why the Church exists and who the Church is to serve.

Some see the Church as a fortress. It is a bastion of strength that stands alone in a hostile world. A place of safety and retreat. Church is where faithful people of God go to be separate from the world. The emphasis is on being secure. If you are faithful, you will act different, look different, dress different, talk different; even have a different diet. There will be certain types of people that you hang around with (people like yourself) and sinners that you will avoid like the plague. The Pharisees held this point of view. They could only recognize Jesus' faithfulness if it fit into the web of regulations that they had teased out of Mosaic legal codes.

> "As Jesus was walking along, he saw a man called Matthew sitting at the tax booth; and he said to him, 'Follow me' and he got up and followed him. And as he sat at dinner in the house, many tax collectors and sinners came and were sitting with him and his disciples. When the Pharisees saw this, they said to his disciples, 'Why does your teacher eat with tax collectors and sinners?'"
>
> Matthew 9:9-11

Pharisees went to great lengths to avoid an unclean object. When you see sin coming, run the other way. Don't support it or lend your approval by your presence or acknowledgment. The Essenes, the religious community that biblical scholars believe John the Baptist came from, built their "fortress" on the northern bank of the Dead Sea. They believed it to be far from the corruption of the rest of humankind.

Christians slip into this withdrawal at times, especially when the sinful lures of the culture seem overpowering. One Christian college was built outside a major city in the late 1800s. The founders believed that it would be eighteen miles from the nearest sin.

John's disciples came to Jesus distraught, "John's disciples, like the disciples of the Pharisees, frequently fast and pray, but your disciples eat and drink" (Luke 5:33). Jesus was too comfortable with the people on the outside. He was too much fun to be spiritual! Jesus was not separate from sinners. He was a friend of sinners. A friend who knew how to have a good time!

The people of God, as Jesus taught, are not to be separate from the world. "Why does your teacher eat with tax collectors and sinners?" Because Jesus came into the world as God's force of love for all humanity, not God's fortress.

"Those who are well have no need of a physician, but those who are sick. Go and learn what this means! I desire mercy, not sacrifice. For I have come to call not the righteous but sinners" (Matthew 9:12-13).

Jesus saw the people of God as a radical spiritual force in the world for the sake of the world. "You are the salt of the earth." What is salt but the flavor, the spice of life! "You are the light of the world. A city built on a hill cannot be hid . . . . In the same way, let your light shine before others, so that they may see your good works and give glory to your Father in heaven" (Matthew 5:13-16). God's people are to be a penetrating force that breaks through the barrier of darkness with the light of God's good news. A force that others will *see, understand*, and then *give* themselves to God as the result.

Jesus sends us out into the world to share the good news with the poor, to proclaim release of the captive and to announce the time of the Lord's favor. He even encourages us to learn from effective models of business and marketing. "Who then is the faithful and prudent manager" (Luke 12:42)?

"See, I am sending you out like sheep into the midst of wolves; so be wise as serpents and innocent as doves" (Matthew 10:16). In this comparison to animal cunning, the serpent stood for everything that was secular and anti-God. The serpent tried to defeat God's purpose in the Garden of Eden. Jesus is implying that we should conduct Kingdom business with the same shrewd principles as the secular world, but with one critical difference. The dove is a symbol of the Spirit—God's presence.[xviii]

We must use the wisdom of the world while we maintain the integrity of the Holy Spirit.

A Place or a People?

People with a fortress mentality tend to assign higher spirituality to a designated place. In the course of his travels, Jesus happened to meet a woman who had probably been excluded from the synagogue (we would say "unchurched") for the better part of her adult life. It had something to do with her self perception and feelings of rejection, associated with the church. She had a string of unsuccessful relationships which included five divorces. The woman asked Jesus an intriguing question. "Where is the right place? My ancestors say right here on this mountain. Your people, the Jews, say that the right place to worship is Jerusalem."[xix]

The Jewish people emphasize a specific place. Jerusalem is the holy city, and the temple in Jerusalem is the holiest place. Holy means to be separate and distinct. What is holy can only be used for one purpose. It is not for common use. There is a clear barrier between secular and sacred. You act differently at home or in your workplace than you would in the temple. You definitely don't play the same music. Keep the coffee and cream outside of the sanctuary! The emphasis is on correct methodology, tradition, and right formulas.

Jesus' emphasis, however, is on people, not place! Truth, not methodology. There is no longer a holy place; only a holy people. "Do you not know that your body is a temple of the Holy Spirit within you, which you have from God, and that you are not your own" (1 Corinthians 6:19)?

There is no longer the clear division between secular truth and sacred truth. If it is true in my home, then it is true at work. If it's true at work, it is true in the church. *All truth is God's truth.* The dividing line of the Age of Reason, between secular and sacred, is blurred. We will use secular music in our worship experience if it gives greater insight into God's truth. Joan Osbourne's song "What

If God Was One Of Us?" has happened! The Word has become flesh and we have experienced God's glory! We dare to play a song that reached number one on the North American music charts, which most unchurched people in our culture recognize, and that asks the ultimate question of reality. Then we preach its fulfillment in Jesus. Lord, help us Jesus, when we pull you off the streets and protect you for ourselves!

One weekend worship theme is "forgiveness." At the end of the message we invite persons forward for an opportunity to forgive those persons who had offended them and to pray for healing. Our worship team was puzzled about an appropriate song to use during this time. We looked through much of the Christian music, but it seems written in a respectable choral language that communicates to older insiders, but not on the street. Instead the band plays the song "Heart of the Matter" by Don Henley, of The Eagles. The song is about a broken relationship, one in which the offending party never says, "I'm sorry," or does anything to right the wrong. The song's message is blunt about forgiveness even when other people don't keep their promises. The number of people who came to the altar for prayer and healing was astonishing and unexpected. Many were unchurched, who through the pain of broken relationships had strong identification with the song every time they heard it on the radio. The words and familiar music bridged their felt need with God's truth and healing power. The Word became flesh. Secular and sacred merged. Life experience intersected with a worship experience that spoke the language of their heart. You call it an *epiphany*. I call it a "God moment" when Awe breaks through into our ordinary experience.

The Apostle Paul understood the importance of meeting people at the place of felt need. Paul met some Epicurean and Stoic philosophers in Athens. They invited Paul to the Areopagus, where many of the scholars would gather to debate.

> "May we know what this new teaching is that you are presenting? It sounds rather strange to us, so we would like to know what it means."
>
> Acts 17:19-20

Paul didn't insult his inquirers. He did not tell them what was wrong with their philosophical or religious perspectives. He simply shared the good news of Jesus Christ in a language that they understood. "For in him we live and move and have our being; as even some of your own poets have said, 'For we too are his offspring'" (Acts 17:28).

Paul does not quote Hebrew Scripture. The Athenians are pre-Christians. They do not understand the language of the Old Testament, but they are familiar with claims about being descendants of the gods. Paul uses secular poetry to communicate our intimate relationship with a personal God! Paul is intentionally inclusive in his choice of communication.

It is a pity that most of the language of the faltering twentieth-century congregation excludes post-modern people.

Leaders with a fortress theology emphasize form and tradition. There is a right way and a wrong way. The Pharisees see Jesus as a Sabbath breaker. He cuts against the grain of the traditional forms.

On a particular Sabbath, Jesus meets a man with a withered hand in the synagogue (Matthew 12:10). The Bible says much about hands. We are to "lift up holy hands" to the Lord. Hands represent our worship. Hands are evidence of our integrity in relationship to God. Jesus talks about "putting our hands to the plow" as a metaphor for God's service. Many people are sitting around our churches with withered, ineffective hands!

Now the Pharisees asked Jesus a question for the purpose of exposing his heresy. "Is it lawful to cure on the Sabbath?" Notice the emphasis on the word *lawful*. Does it follow the right traditional form? You know what we mean. Are you doing it according to the rule book? Is it constitutional?

Jesus doesn't have a fortress theology. His emphasis is not on place, form, methodology, or tradition. Jesus' focus is on the well-being of people. "Suppose one of you has only one sheep and it falls into a pit on the Sabbath; will you not lay hold of it and lift it out? How much more valuable is a human being than a sheep! So it is lawful to do good on the Sabbath!"

Do you hear what Jesus is saying? It is not about doing things the way church regulators have been doing things in the past. It is not about sacred space, days, or traditions. You do whatever it takes to bring wellness to people in Jesus' name. If someone is in a hole of depression, you don't ask if it is secular or sacred music. If coffee in the sanctuary puts people in a more receptive mood to encounter God's love, then you have coffee in the sanctuary. *Jesus meets people where they are for the purpose of healing and transformation.*

> "Then he said to the man, 'Stretch out your hand.' He stretched it out, and it was restored, as sound as the other. But the Pharisees went out and conspired against him, how to destroy him."
>
> Matthew 12:9-14

The ineffective hand was made effective. Many of our churches stand in the way of healing because we want stability and privacy instead. Our traditions limit the potential of what God wants to do. We end up working against Jesus. What is the right thing to do? Whatever it takes to get people out of the pit. Helping people become whole through an encounter with Jesus Christ in a language that they understand.

Has the incarnate God moved into your neighborhood? How can you tell?

Chapter 3:

Wineskins change!

"New wine is not put into old wineskins; otherwise,
the skins burst, and the wine is spilled, and the skins
are destroyed; but new wine is put into fresh wineskins,
and so both are preserved."[xx]
Matthew 9:17, Jesus

Jesus agreed to become human among religious people who resisted change. "The disciples of John came to him, saying, 'Why do we and the Pharisees fast often, but your disciples do not fast'" (Matthew 9:14)? Translation: "Why are you using different methods than the methods we have always used in the past?"

> "The Pharisees and scribes came to Jesus from Jerusalem and said, 'Why do your disciples break the tradition of the elders? For they do not wash their hands before they eat.'" He answered them, 'And why do you break the commandment of God for the sake of your tradition?'"
>
> Matthew 15:1-3

People who were trying to honor God were actually standing in God's way. Since its inception, the Church remains one of the most resistant organizations in the world, when it comes to change. Our stubbornness, which amounts to a "hardening of the heart," is ironic because we follow a God who is continually doing new things. "I am about to do a new thing; now it springs forth, do you not perceive it" (Isaiah 43:19)? We follow a living God, an active God, a God who is on the move.

The Tabernacle is a wonderful model of God's presence in the lives of God's people.[xxi] The design was given to Moses by God. The key factor in the design was its mobility. God is not a God who stays in one place. God is on the move! Our challenge is to follow in obedience to the places of promise that are as yet unknown. We are to be a pilgrim people. People who are always on the move. The journey ahead is perilous. There are giant obstacles that lie in the path that can never be overcome in our own strength or resources. If we are willing to take the risk, God will make a way. But we must never stop and stay where we are!

"New wine must be put into fresh wineskins." My mentor, Howard Snyder, said it so well:

"Every age knows the temptation to forget that the gospel is ever new. We try to contain the new wine of the gospel in old wineskins—outmoded tradition, obsolete philosophies, creaking institutions, old habits. But with time the old wineskins begin to bind the gospel. Then they must burst, and the power of the gospel pours forth once more. Many times this has happened in the history of the Church. Human nature wants to conserve, but the divine nature is to renew. It seems almost a law that things initially created to aid the gospel eventually become obstacles—old wineskins."[xxii]

Our people often resist change because they fail to differentiate between the wine and the wineskins. They confuse core values with cultural practices.

James Collins, author of *Built To Last: Successful Habits of Visionary Companies,*[xxiii] helped me get a better understanding of this principle.

The core values of the Church, the wine, are the constant. The core values of the Church are the mandates of our Lord that we cannot compromise.

"All authority in heaven and on earth has been given to me (The Lordship of Jesus Christ). Go therefore and make disciples of all nations, baptizing them in the name of the Father and of the Son and of the Holy Spirit, and teaching them to obey everything that I have commanded you. And remember, I am with you always, to the end of the age."

Matthew 28:18-20

core values

"I give you a new commandment, that you love one another. Just as I have loved you, you also should love one another. By this everyone will know that you are my disciples, if you have love for one another."

John 13:34-35

You have power with God by your actions toward people. Especially poor and disenfranchised people. Jesus told a young entrepreneur who inquired about spiritual well-being. "There is still one thing that you lack. Sell all that you own and distribute the money to the poor, and you will have treasure in heaven; then come, follow me" (Luke 9:18-20). Many of us have conveniently reduced this core value to a cultural practice. You cannot follow the Spirit of God and fail to go where God is going. An unchangeable core value: "the poor have the good news brought to them" (Matthew 11:5).

The core values and purposes of the church do not change. These are the values for which the saints of God willingly give their lives. *Core values are not market driven!* There are times when the church

See CD ROM: *Multi-sensory Worship*

"Walter George/Danny, Danny's mom, Migrant workers"

must get smaller because we are not willing to trade truth for relevancy. Core purpose doesn't change, but the way you practice it, or live it, must change.

It is easy to confuse core values with cultural practices. On December 17, 1994 Ginghamsburg Church moved from our tiny campus, where people had gathered since 1876, to a modern, 100-acre campus with 60,000 square feet of space. We joined the Media Reformation that weekend. The high-tech equipment was a novelty that none of

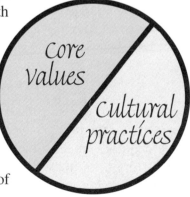

us really knew how to use. For the first six months we were fortunate if the presentation was in focus! The opposition, rather muffled at first, grew louder.

"This doesn't seem like Ginghamsburg Church anymore. It looks like a slick production." And "We've changed. We are not committed to the same truths anymore!"

Yes, we did change. We changed our methodology in worship for the sake of remaining true to our unchangeable core value: unchurched people matter to God! We acknowledged the value of 99:1. "Which of you, having a hundred sheep and losing one of them, does not leave the ninety-nine in the wilderness and go after the one that is lost until he finds it" (Luke 15:4)?

Having a worship experience that bridges unchurched personal needs with God's presence is a core value. We commit ourselves to a contemporary worship style. The core value doesn't change. **But contemporary for 1979 is not contemporary in the 1990s.** When some churches talk about beginning a contemporary worship experience, they mean "forward into the 1970s"!

Our sacred practices ought to be challenged. You can't put the new thing that God is doing in old wineskins. Sacred practices are not always the same as core values!

We ask repeatedly "What are the core values for our church?" Everything else is open to change. We are careful not to allow growth and the use of technology to pull us away from who we are. Growth can make preserving the core a much harder task. The point of correction is to remember that the medium is not the message: It's the wineskin.

Four Communication/ Technology Shifts

Oral Storytelling

Storytelling was the methodology for communication used by Jesus. It was the primary means of communication through the first three centuries of the Church. The method is parabolic, based on visual stories that were driven by contemporary experience.

"Which one of you having a hundred sheep"

"There was a man who had two sons"

"Or what woman having ten silver coins"

Jesus wasn't telling 2000-year-old stories. He was bridging common, everyday experiences with God's possibilities.

"Picture the lilies of the field"

"Look at that fig tree"

Oral storytelling makes ample use of visual imagery and contemporary experience. It is not abstract and cerebral. "Tell me a story, Mommy"

Tex Sample tells about the struggle he had when he first went to college. "You see, I had come out of an oral culture. My world was not one of discourse, systematic coherence, the consistent use of clear definitions, and the writing of discursive prose that could withstand the whipsaws of academic critique. Rather, it was a world made sense of through proverbs, stories, and relationships. A great deal of what we knew was tacitly understood . . . . We knew things we couldn't say, we felt things we couldn't name, and we did things we couldn't explain. So proverbs and stories helped us. They pointed to what we meant."[xxiv]

Stories help us understand who we are. My grandfather died in August of 1996. His picture sits across the room from where I sit as I write this book. He taught me much about faith and life. Even though he had only an eighth-grade education, he played a major role in helping me become who I am today. I loved to go to my grandparents' home in the summer. I yearn to hear the stories that they would tell on their front porch. We went on many fishing trips together. I learned how to find night crawlers, bait a hook, hold and clean a fish. In the oral culture, you learn by doing, through apprenticeship. In the literate age, you learn in the classroom and by reading.

I caught something more important than fish by those rural ponds of Kentucky. Through my grandfather's storytelling I learned about my past. How my ancestor came from England in the 1700s. He married an American woman and had two sons. Both sons became ministers; one a Baptist, the other a Methodist. Perhaps we hear God's voice through storytelling, because my cousin, Daryl Docterman, became a Baptist minister.

Alex Haley shared with us the powerful method of storytelling for the purpose of transmitting cultural values and identity in the epic story of "Roots". The story of his ancestral Mandinka village in Africa and his ancestor Kunta Kinte was orally passed from one generation to another.

My grandfather's wise proverb still speaks to me when I am tempted to be prideful. "Son, never forget who made you!" In the oral tradition our world picture is formed through storytelling, proverbs and relationships.

Manuscript

When Christianity became the state religion under the Emperor Constantine in the fourth century, more emphasis was placed upon the need for an "official" canon. Christian writings become canonical when recognized as authoritative, for what we believe and how we live. Various splinter groups were beginning to formulate their own authoritative canons. Some were being led astray. As the Church moved farther away from the apostles and early Church leaders, the need grew for authoritative records.

The individual books and letters of the New Testament had been used and recognized by the Church for many years. Tertullian referred to the Christian writing as the New Testament around 220.[xxv] The leaders of the Church met in Carthage (397) and formally affirmed the twenty-seven books of the New Testament. Athanasius, the bishop of Alexandria, listed in an Easter letter of 367, the same twenty-seven books that we now have in the New Testament as canonical.[xxvi]

From this point until the Protestant Reformation, we tend to find Bibles chained to the altars of churches. A major cathedral might only have one. Bibles were incredibly expensive because they were produced by hand. A scribe went through the lengthy, artistic process of hand writing each individual letter. The project could take as long as two years. "Look but don't touch" was the attitude of the day. The Bible was not for the common person. Most people couldn't read. The reader became an important player in this scenario. The lay reader is still part of the worship experience in some of our traditions. Memorization was developed as a primary educational discipline. The only Bible most people had was the Bible in their head. The manuscript era was still a pre-literate culture. The shift from storyteller to reader was not a radical change.

Mass Print

Christians evolve in the communication of faith with each new innovation in communication technology. Johannes Gutenberg's invention of the printing press (circa 1440-1456) brought a radical paradigm shift to the way people did church. The shift met with much resistance. "How can you take something holy and produce it in large quantities through secular technology?" Early pioneers are always considered heretics.

Martin Luther's translation of the Bible from Latin to German was to be produced in large enough quantities that the cost to the reader went down. The Bible was no longer a book only for the few, privileged, literate persons of means. The chain on the altar was broken. The Book was now readily available to the masses. Luther's entrepreneurship actually fanned the flames of literacy. The Bible and catechisms developed around the Bible became the primers through which people learned to read.

> "When printing was invented, the Church changed its way of functioning. It did not take the printed word into the heart of its oral culture but rather let that culture disappear and replaced it, in its pastoral program, with the catechism and the school system."[xxvii]

The age of literacy was a shift from visual imagery, feeling, and contemporary experience to abstract and cerebral thinking. Disciplines that grew out of the classroom (systematic theology, biblical criticism, and the emphasis on doctrinal distinctives) consumed the focus of Church leadership.

Mass print became a vehicle that brought the good news of Jesus Christ to millions of persons. But a literate congregation also required a movement to a more cerebral form of faith that was filled with doctrines and abstract formulas of correctness. Definition and rationalistic explanation replaced mystery. This paralleled the secular Age of Enlightenment and the movement to rationalism.

Many confused the wineskin with the wine, and the Church lost much of the experience of awe and wonder that comes through the Holy Spirit.

Electronic Media

Experience is back! From remote control, to surround sound, to home entertainment systems, we are a visual, multi-sensory, emotive culture. We don't just see and hear. We want to feel what we hear. The boom box, carried on the shoulder and pressed against the ear, was enhanced with maximum bass response. The same effect has been reproduced in much smaller disc players with head phones. How do you judge quality? You feel it through maximum bass. Speakers, wattage, and size are major considerations when making a stereo purchase. Systems are getting smaller and more powerful at the same time.

The TV remote control has changed the way we learn. I don't watch one channel at a time. The Sports Channel, a movie and CNN can hold my attention at the same time. Sometimes I find myself doing nothing more than grazing through 76 channels in the process of half an hour. It's amazing what I can learn about home decorating, the environment, travel, old movies, world events and religion in 30 minutes. I make a decision in less than 4 seconds to change the channel on my TV or the radio station in my car. Our short attention spans have caused TV producers to use rapid fire edits. Watch "NYPD Blue" or "MTV" and count—. . . one thousand one . . . one thousand two . . .—almost all edits are less than 4 seconds.

We shall fail in communicating Jesus to this generation with 60 minutes of literate-linear worship. Watching a "talking head" for 30 minutes of lecture is a futile exercise.

Multi-sensory experiences are mandatory! Last summer my son and I went to Florida where he participated in a week long baseball camp. We decided to go a couple of days early and do the "Disney thing." Jonathan had never been. I had put it off because I can think of better places to spend my time than hot, crowded amusement parks. But it was time to fulfill my parental responsibility. I was shocked. We had an incredible time; we stayed from dawn until dusk. It was an experience! From the time you get in line you become a participant in a multi-sensory electronic media adventure. You feel the alien's breath, the drip of saliva, the vibration of his steps. You see the ghostly appearance of holograms riding with you in the car. **When is the last time you went to church and wanted to stay all day?**

Why is media a life or death issue for the Church? Whoever controls the media controls the values and direction of the post-modern culture; a media-driven culture where children kill children for Michael Jordan gym shoes (valued at $125) and learn their sexual values from "Baywatch." Who will define reality in a virtual-reality world that goes from Barney the purple dinosaur to babies dying in Rwanda at the push of a remote control button? Will sadistic movies like "Pulp Fiction" and "Natural Born Killers" define humor for post-moderns?

> "When the day of Pentecost had come . . . all of them
> were filled with the Holy Spirit and began to speak in
> other languages, as the Spirit gave them ability."
>
> Acts 2:4

Followers of Jesus were given the ability by God to communicate in the contemporary language of the culture. Electronic media are much more than entertainment.

Carolyn and I took our children to Steven Spielberg's movie "Schindler's List" when it was first released. The movie is based on the story about a Catholic business man who used all of his resources to buy the freedom of concentration camp prisoners in Nazi Germany. Some viewers would call this merely "entertainment." It is much more than entertainment. The movie is multi-sensory communication that is created for the purpose of transformation. I urged my children to see the horror of human potential and give themselves more fully to the alternative purposes of the Kingdom of God. The multi-sensory communication art of film would do more for them in 2-1/2 hours than anything they would ever read in a book.

Electronic media are a life or death issue for the Church because electronic media are the language of our culture.

Part Two

A Post-modern Strategy for the Third Millennium church

Introduction: Celebration, Cell, and Call

The journey with Jesus is a journey to wellness. God's purpose is to transform each one of us into the fully integrated personality who is found in Jesus. Jesus is what it looks like to be human according to God's design. The first Adam is the illustration of human dysfunction.

> "They heard the sound of the Lord God walking in
> the garden at the time of the evening breeze, and the
> man and his wife hid themselves from the presence of
> the Lord God among the trees of the garden."
>
> Genesis 3:8

When God becomes hidden, your concept of self and your relationships with others become distorted. How did the demonic institution of slavery exist in a civilized culture that claimed to be Christian? When God is hidden in a person's life, distorted, evil human behaviors result:

- holocaust—6 million human beings exterminated because they were Jewish
- apartheid in South Africa
- racist and sexist views that still exist in much of the Church
- adultery
- abortion—the casual attitude that our culture takes toward abortion as a means of birth control
- divorce rates which have resulted in one out of three children in North America not being raised in a home with both parents.

Like Cain, who murdered his brother Abel, you lose all sense of what it means to be a child of God who is responsible for "being my brother's and sister's keeper." Life becomes self-centered instead of God-centered. All sense of divine purpose is lost. You give yourself fully to making a living but end up failing to fully live.

Jesus, the second Adam, is the visual demonstration of humanity made whole.

> "I do nothing on my own, but I speak these things as
> the Father instructed me and the one who sent me is
> with me; he has not left me alone, for I always do what
> is pleasing to him."
>
> John 8:28-29

Wholeness comes from a vital relationship with God and the commitment to "always do what is pleasing to him." The journey with Jesus is a transformational experience to wholeness.

Relationships and journeys do not happen in the sterile, abstract catechisms and liturgies that are often associated with church models of the literate age. People are not looking for information about God. They want to experience God as Paul encountered the risen Christ on the Damascus Road.

> "While I was on my way and approaching Damascus,
> about noon a great bright light from heaven suddenly
> shone about me. I fell to the ground and heard a voice
> saying to me . . . I answered 'Who are you, Lord?' Then
> he said to me 'I am Jesus of Nazareth'"
>
> Acts 22:6-8

Post-moderns live out of a sense of rhythm, vibration, and experience. Dolby "surround sound" systems once experienced only in movie theaters are being built into our homes. Where we once had only televisions, we now have complex "home entertainment centers" with more remote controls than we can possibly use.

Information will no longer suffice. Have you noticed the way that new programming is being reformatted? NBC has started a trend that the other networks are beginning to follow.

"Under the guidance of news president Andrew Lack who took over NBC's news division in 1993, the NBC Nightly News has had a remarkable makeover: fewer stories per night, moving the broadcast closer to a magazine-show approach; less traditional news from Washington and more on user-friendly topics like health, the family and consumer issues, and a jazzier format, with lots of catch labels for continuing segments. Brokaw now stands, rather than sits, in front of a very '90's video wall . . . . NBC stories are more likely to go for the gut and the pop-cultural hot button."[xxviii]

Has NBC lost sight of their original mission?

"'The mission of the program remains identical,' says Lack. 'That is to bring the best execution journalistically of the most important news of the day. I don't think our program is better than World News Tonight or the CBS Evening News with Dan Rather. But we made a conscious effort to produce a somewhat different program from the ones they do.' It's a more 'populist' approach, he concedes, which eschews Washington 'process' stories—subcommittee hearings, presidential speeches—in favor of 'the real news in people's lives.'"[xxix]

NBC has been able to make the important distinction between core values that stay the same and cultural practice that is continually changing in favor of the "real news in people's lives."

Our post-modern strategy for the third millennium Church must move beyond the abstract, cerebral models of the literate age. Our strategy will bridge the truth of God's Gospel with the felt needs in people's lives.

The strategy of transformation that we have committed ourselves to at Ginghamsburg Church is to involve people in the life rhythm of Celebration, Cell, and Call.

Chapter 4

celebration

"But the hour is come, and is now here, when the true worshipers will worship the Father in spirit and in truth, for the Father seeks such as these to worship him. God is spirit, and those who worship him must worship in spirit and truth."
John 4:23-24

Worship is the single most important act of human existence. Worship means "worth." We worship whatever has ultimate worth and value in our lives.

True worship is not measured by style, location, or methodology. True worship happens when Spirit touches spirit. When God's Spirit touches human spirit, people become aware of the reality of God's presence and they recommit themselves to live lifestyles of Godly integrity. Priorities are realigned. Ultimate values are clarified and reaffirmed. The answers to life's basic questions—Where did we come from? Why are we here? Where are we going?—are brought to a fully conscious level in our thinking. Worship is a movement from illusion to reality. We are reminded that there is a God and that we are not God. We cannot live by bread alone but must depend upon every word that comes from God's mouth. Every moment of life is a gift from God's hand, and we can only find fulfillment as we live each moment in God's hand. Spirit (presence) and Truth (integrity) are what we gather to remember each week.

Reality check. True worship shakes our world view and reminds us of the radical, counter-culture values of the Kingdom of God. We are reminded that the core of life is not matter but Spirit.

Faith and focus. Effective worship brings us to that "ah ha!" moment. Worship restores the "wow" factor in our lives. This is what life is all about! It's not running the rat race at an ever-increasing pace or owning a bigger house or more expensive car; wearing designer clothes or retiring at age fifty. Life is found in Jesus Christ . . . It's about living God's purpose . . . serving people . . . and keeping my promises.

Oh how easy it is to forget these truths during the drop-dead deadlines of the work week, family time demands, and ever-increasing economic challenges of life in the dawn of a new millennium.

When God's Spirit touches my spirit, I am reminded that success does not necessarily equal wholeness.

Let me point out what should be obvious. A worship service might not necessarily involve true worship. True worship is Spirit touching spirit. Worship happens when the presence of God is bridged with people's felt needs in their life context.

Post-moderns have a deep felt need to be anchored in a spiritual reality. The writer-futurist Faith Popcorn, who consults with many Fortune 500 companies, including American Express, Eastman Kodak, IBM, and Procter & Gamble, speaks on this trend of spirituality.

"Anchoring is a new trend, and it's enormous. It's everything from wearing a little angel to burning incense to doing yoga. That's the reason why Zen Buddhism and alternative religions are growing—and even more versions of the Christian religion."[xxx]

As we approach the year 2000, there is a growing spiritual restlessness. Will the Church of Jesus Christ be able to effectively communicate Jesus as God's answer to a culture asking spiritual questions? If we are going to connect we must deal with people's real questions. How do we communicate the gospel to a media generation that "sees" in images? As Robert Duffett so effectively states, "The language, thought and ideas of the Bible may be so foreign to secularized Western culture that contemporary communicators become missionaries in their own culture. Like missionaries attempting to communicate the Christian faith 'cross-culturally,' contemporary communicators must accept the way understanding is embodied in language. If not, all efforts at communication will be meaningless and ineffective. We must find cultural references (connections) that enable the communication of Biblical teaching. When the Biblical message is communicated in the language and thought forms of the people, it has the highest probability of connecting with listeners."[xxxi]

Electronic media are the language of our culture. Our strategies for designing worship must be visually engaging.

Back To The Future: Designing Worship Celebrations for a Post-literate Age

"To accomplish its mission, religious leadership will use media to tell stories of the faith: creative leaders of the future will develop media literacy."[xxxii]

Leonard Sweet

How do you design a worship experience in a post-literate age where about 100 percent of the North American culture receives most information from a source other than the printed text? We need to go back to the future by asking "How did the Church do worship in a pre-literate culture?"

The pre-literate Church made rich use of visual imagery. The medieval churches in Europe depended upon the visual arts to tell the biblical story. Elaborate wood and stone carvings, massive stained glass windows, tapestries, frescoes, and detailed paintings by the masters mixed with dramas that were often used as interludes in the sermons. This appeal to the senses made the Church the best multi-media experience in town. Candles and incense added to the multi-sensory environment. The ritual, with "bells and smells," was intentionally designed as pictures for the senses.

"The visual arts were so central to the presentation of the gospel in the middle ages that they even influenced the ways preachers spoke and gestured! Late-medieval preachers were skilled visual performers who used a repertoire of gestures known to their audiences from paintings. Manuals of such gestures existed, providing a stylized body language that accompanied and heightened the verbal communication."[xxxiii]

The contemporary secular technology, the pipe organ, was incorporated into the communication strategy of the medieval Church and had astounding success in its impact upon reaching the unchurched. It probably comes as no surprise—the godfathers and godmothers of the Church strongly resisted the use of a secular instrument in a holy place. "We've never done it that way before!"

We live in an age where text, audio, and video converge into the new mixed genre, which is labeled *multi-media*.[xxxiv] This convergence drives us back to the future to design worship experiences that are tactile and multi-sensory. Traditional, abstract liturgy no longer speaks the language of a post-modern culture. Our worship forms must bridge a person's mind to connect to feelings and emotions. Pre-literate worship centers evoked awe and wonderment. Electronic media are no longer an option for the church. Electronic media are the language of our culture.

See CD ROM: *Multi-sensory Worship*

Electronic media

Ginghamsburg Church joined the Media Reformation on December 17, 1994. Media becomes part of every worship experience. Worship attendance grew from 1,200 to over 3,100 in the first two and a half years. Almost half of the people who have come to the church during that time were unchurched.

We use electronic media in an interactive form with music, literature, painting, drama, dance, writing, filmmaking, poetry and movie clips. We borrow ideas from David Letterman's "almost live" spots, in which he appears to leave the studio by playing clips that are really produced earlier. With this tactic I am able to go "on location" in the middle of my sermon. Electronic media open the door to unlimited creative possibilities.

It All Starts on Wednesday Morning

8:00 a.m.

The Celebration Team (Worship Design Team) gathers in a small conference room, equipped with ideas, music CDs, and plenty of coffee. Their purpose is to design the upcoming weekend worship experience. The team includes:

1. **Creative Coordinator**, who directs and coordinates the entire creative process from music group leaders, dramas, staging, writing calls to worship, prayers, segues, and announcements.

2. **Technical Coordinator**, who directs and coordinates the technical process from lighting to sound. This person acts as a floor director during the worship celebration and is in constant communication with lighting, sound and video support. This person runs the technical rehearsal every Saturday afternoon.

3. **Communications Director**, who has a marketing background and understands the principles of advertising. This person is in charge of all communication strategies for the church. Three or more times per year this person plans and develops advertising campaigns for celebration events which are announced in TV, radio, Internet, and newspaper spots. This person's most important role on the team is to help it identify and speak to the felt need of the culture each week.

4. **Multi-Media Director,** who is the video guru who oversees all video production and computer graphic presentations during the celebration event.

5. **Band Leader,** who is (preferably) a professional or trained musician. The band leader absorbs ideas from Wednesday, arranges music, selects musicians, rehearses music with music team(s) and choir(s) on Thursday evening and Saturday afternoon and then goes live at the worship celebration on Saturday evening by 5:30 p.m. Amazing!

6. **Lead Pastor (and support pastor if a multi-staff church).**

The lead pastor speaks at weekend worship celebrations approximately 36 to 38 weekends a year. The support pastor speaks at other celebrations, or directs an alternative celebration for Gen X worship (for persons who are twentysomething, and born well after 1964). This pastor's primary responsibility is to bring a basic idea or direction for the weekend's message to the meeting each Wednesday morning.

8:00—8:30 a.m.

The team discusses the previous weekend's worship experience. What worked? What didn't work? What were the technical flaws that need correction? What can we learn from this experience to make ourselves and our worship more pleasing to God? The expectation of excellence in worship is non-negotiable. Lyle Shaller's research has shown North Americans to be "increasingly unforgiving of mediocrity, incompetence, malfeasance or an inability to adopt to a new era. The call today is for high performance."[xxxv]

The celebration team shares personal issues and talks about what they are learning through prayer and meditation. Renewal is breathed upon us by God, not programmed and planned. (I spend at least an hour or more in prayer Wednesday morning before I come to the celebration meeting. Often I have fasted the day before.)

8:30—10:00 a.m.

The lead pastor introduces the seed idea that is germinating in his or her spiritual life, or in the congregation. Grace, doubt, faith, struggle, integrity, relationships—the idea grows out of the lead pastor's life experience and personal relationship with God. Most often it is linked to a Scripture verse. The team works with the idea and most importantly they identify the felt need that connects with the seeker. (See the list of basic felt needs.)

"The only messages that will reach seekers are ones that connect to relevant life issues. It is not that seekers are selfish. Rather, most are 'running on empty' and look to messages to give them hope, courage, inspiration, or perspective. Communicators must learn the art and skill of connection."[xxxvi] The celebration team spends more than an hour working the connection. The lead pastor comes away energized with great ideas, illustrations, and content to use in the message. Often relevant movie clips are identified at this point.

The Basic Felt Needs

"making a connection with personal experience in worship"

➤ **Belonging** The need to be a part of something bigger than yourself; such as family, heritage, and involvement.

➤ **Love** The need to express and experience unconditional love. Acceptance, forgiveness, and a second chance are each components of love.

➤ **Identity** The need to understand oneself and one's place in the world; such as self reflection, learning from mistakes, and meaning.

➤ **"Possibilization"** The need and anticipation that our conditions or ourselves will be bettered in the future. This concept is described by such words as winning, achievement, making a difference, and hope.

➤ **Freedom** The need to have restrictions or obstacles removed from our path. Leisure, simplicity, wholeness, and security are each related to freedom.

➤ **Authenticity** The need to be true to ourselves through integrity, consistency, and honesty.

10:00—11:00 a.m. The Elements of Design

There are six elements of worship design to identify and extend each week.

word:	The word of God, as discerned in the Scripture.
felt need:	the presenting need(s) that the people bring to worship
desired outcome:	the expected responses that people will make
theme:	the package in which the message is wrapped
metaphor:	the root image which permits the desired outcome to connect with the needs of the people
structure:	the order of worship

It is difficult to overemphasize the importance of identifying a strong metaphor. Metaphors are bridges that help a person understand the relevance of Gospel truth. Jesus made ample use of metaphors. "The kingdom of heaven is like a mustard seed that someone took and sowed in his field" (Matthew 13:31). He used this metaphor on several occasions to make different points. "For truly I tell you, if you have faith the size of a mustard seed, you will say to this mountain, 'Move from here to there' and it will move; and nothing will be impossible for you" (Matthew 17:20).

The theme for one summer weekend might be "traveling companions." The intent is to communicate the importance of Christian community and emphasize the second critical part of our strategy for transformation: involvement in cell (small group ministry). The Yellow Brick Road from *The Wizard of Oz* becomes the metaphor. Yellow bricks are stacked on the altar table. The band plays a jazz rendition of "Somewhere Over The Rainbow" for a prelude, followed by a brief movie clip of Dorothy and her three unlikely traveling companions on the journey to find home. The worship host follows the movie clip with this call to worship:

> "You and I are on a journey too. And even though we're human beings, we also frequently suffer from incompleteness. Empty hearts, fried brains, emotional homelessness. We know where to go for help but the journey is seldom easy and was never meant to be a solo act. The word for tonight/today: **DO NOT ATTEMPT THIS ALONE.**
>
> We come to worship as a group. To do it a thousand times better than any one of us could worship alone. For Jesus said where several of us are gathered in his name, he is there in the middle. Let's stand to sing and enjoy his presence together."

The drama and the message equated the Christian journey to the four traveling companions and the obstacles that would confront them along the way. Dorothy, the Lion, Tin Man, and Scarecrow would have never reached their destination alone. They needed each other. Acts 4:32-37 is the text:

"Now the whole group of those who believed were of one heart and soul, and no one claimed private ownership of any possessions, but everything they owned was held in common . . . There was not a needy person among them, for as many as owned lands or houses sold them and brought the proceeds of what was sold."

The text suggests the Barnabas principle: becoming sons and daughters of encouragement. What does *The Wizard of Oz* have to do with this passage? Christians are on a journey. Our destination is the city of God. It is a journey that you dare not attempt alone. Obstacles lie in wait. There are forces at work that will attempt to keep you from reaching home.

Following the worship celebrations persons are invited to visit tables set up in the entry ways where they can receive information about cell ministry. Worship develops into commitment and personal action when we identify a strong root metaphor and grow the experience around it.

11:00—12:00 noon Structure

The room is a mess by this time. The walls are covered with newsprint that is lined with ideas. Four pots of coffee, granola bars and various other edibles have been consumed. The team has identified felt need, desired outcome, and theme. The metaphor has been chosen. They are now ready to outline the structure of the upcoming weekend's worship experience. It's time to identify the music that they will use according to the theme and metaphor. This usually involves a prelude, two or three songs for congregational singing, special music done at the time of offering, a choir number (choral music is performed at worship celebrations, except for Gen X services, at least twice a month) and a closing musical transition. The team works in creative chaos, listening to CDs, and using the Internet to find songs that are mentioned while brainstorming. The music coordinator usually brings some ideas for congregational singing that he has thought about previously. The technical coordinator builds the outline for the weekend worship celebration on the whiteboard.

Structure for the Worship Celebration

Opening Music *Band:* Instrumental, "Somewhere Over the Rainbow"

Opening Video Clip *Multi-media Coordinator: The Wizard of Oz (two-minute segment, which includes Dorothy agreeing to go forward with her 3 new companions; encountering danger)*

Call To Worship *Creative Coordinator: (from center platform; based on the idea of not traveling alone)*

Song Celebration *Band:* "Love Is What We've Come Here For"

"We've Come to Praise You" *(congregational songs led by the band, with words projected on the screen)*

Prayer *Creative Coordinator: (soft music underscores a prayer which gives us the opportunity to pray for others who will journey with us)*

Brief Reprise *Band:* "Surely the Presence of the Lord"

Bridge/Offering *Creative Coordinator: (a connecting piece which calls the ushers and affirms community)*

Featured Music *Band:* "I'll Be There For You" *(as the theme song for the TV show "Friends," this Cranberries' tune reaches out to younger people in the congregation, as well as carrying the theme for the weekend forward)*

Drama *Troupe: Four "Buster-type" persons, who resemble (in both looks and mannerisms) the characters of the Wizard of Oz, wrestle with the challenges of community in a coffee-house setting.*

Message *Lead Pastor:* "Traveling Companions"

Closing Words *Creative Coordinator*

Send Out *Band:* "I'll Be There For You"

12:00 Noon

The team agrees upon the worship structure, and each team member sets out to work on individual tasks until they meet together again as an entire team on Saturday evening at 5:00. Meanwhile the intense work begins.

The creative coordinator writes the call to worship, prayer, drama, and connecting pieces. She recruits a worship host, drama cast and works with the band leader in coordinating music functions. She guides the design of the drama set, altar decorations, and tactile room symbols that will be completed and in place by 4:15 p.m. on Saturday afternoon. She oversees two drama rehearsals.

The *multi-media coordinator* builds the story board and coordinates all video and computer graphics production for the weekend.

The band leader recruits musicians, arranges music, and rehearses with the band and choir on Thursday evening and Saturday afternoon.

The technical coordinator ties together all of the loose ends, including arranging interviews and going on video shoots with the multimedia coordinator.

The *pastor* is working on the sermon. The creative coordinator and pastor will touch base three or four times between Wednesday afternoon and Friday morning to make sure that sermon, drama, and worship theme are all tracking together. The team keeps working the process. Don't let it go! Keep making it better! You can even change the metaphor as late as Friday afternoon if it is not communicating the intended message. The final draft of the sermon is done by Friday morning at 11:30.

Friday, 11:30 a.m.—12:30 p.m.

The Micro Team (creative coordinator, technical coordinator, and multi-media coordinator) meet with the pastor. The pastor rehearses the message with this group. They tell the pastor what works and what doesn't make sense. They have liberty to make cuts on the pastor's message! They make the message better. The team discusses further ways to support the message visually through images that will appear on the twenty-foot screen throughout the message. Original artwork will be generated on a computer by a staff graphic artist, in addition to video spots and interviews, movie clips, and pictures that come from books, magazines, and newspapers, which are scanned into the computer and later projected on the screen.

Friday Afternoon

The multi-media team goes to work on visualizing the weekend message.

9:00 p.m.

The multi-media coordinator leaves the office. But one light still burns bright. The graphic artist is often not done until after midnight. What commitment! The message on behalf of Jesus is important business!

Saturday Afternoon 2:00 p.m.

The pastor arrives at the office for an important time of centering and prayer. This business of communication is taxing. The pastor cannot stand before the people at 5:30 without this time of reflection and prayer. The worship center is already energized by the activity of the music and drama teams' preparations as the pastor enters the building.

3:45 p.m. Multi-media/Sermon Technical Rehearsal

The pastor meets with the multi-media coordinator and the technical coordinator, who will be the floor director, and the weekend video director who is an unpaid servant. They rehearse the sermon and synchronize it for the first time with computer video and graphic support on the computer screen. They make corrections. The sermon is transposed into a technical form to be used by unpaid servants. (As many as 100 people can be involved in a rotating schedule throughout the year in this type of media ministry.) These servants will run sound, lights, cameras, computer, projectors, and switches.

See CD ROM: *Multi-sensory Worship*

The pastor moves aside for more prayer. "Lord help me. I have no power or strength in myself."

4:15 p.m. Main Sanctuary

The technical coordinator runs the technical rehearsal from A to Z. Sound, video, and camera checks are tested on each part. If something is not working and can't be corrected, it is pulled. *It is better not to do something than do it badly!*

5:00 p.m.

The last meeting is in the small conference room before God's people appear. The Wednesday morning worship design team is back together again along with the unpaid servants who will direct, work lights, sound, music, and host the celebration event. The technical coordinator hands out the final worship script, and they go through it together.

See CD ROM: *Multi-sensory Worship*

"Easter Script"

"Any questions?" Most importantly, they pray.

"God, we are your servants. We thank you for the opportunity to be used for your purpose. We have done the best that we know how. Take our limited efforts and let people see Jesus. Do it God!"

5:30 p.m. Lights Up—Worship Alive!

See CD ROM: *Multi-sensory Worship*

"Easter Script"

(with call to worship, etc., and last week Easter review)

6:35 p.m.

The team meets in a music room for the purpose of evaluation. What works? What doesn't work? Keep working and reworking the process. Parts of the sermon during the first service are changed. Lines in the drama are clarified; technical corrections are made.

7:00 p.m. Worship Celebration 2

9:00 p.m. The team heads home.

Sunday 8:00 a.m.
The team meets to go over worship script and changes. Again, we pray!

8:30 a.m.
Worship Celebration 3

9:45 a.m.
Worship Celebration 4

11:15 a.m.
Worship Celebration 5

6:00 p.m. Souljourn, A Worship Experience for Generation X
The worship team that is responsible for the celebration experiences end their work week by 1:00 p.m. on Sunday. None of them are involved on a week-to-week basis with the Gen X celebration. The Gen X team operates in a very similar way with similar functions as those outlined above. There is one exception at Ginghamsburg. Every member of the Gen X worship team, with the exception of the Gen X pastor, is an unpaid servant.

The effective worship team of the twenty-first century church will function much like the production team of a weekly magazine formatted news program. The teams that produce *20/20* and *Prime-time Live* persevere in high pressure, tight timelines, and demand for excellent work. The editorial teams that produce *USA Today* and *The Globe and Mail* in Canada have to turn out a new product five times a week!

A post-literate strategy for worship will radically redefine church staffing. Will seminaries be major players in the church of the twenty-first century? Not unless they make the paradigm shift from literate to post-literate culture. The effective churches that have made the shift will become the seminaries that staff the church of tomorrow. Many staff recruits will come directly from the corporate world. This probability becomes more intriguing as aging baby boomers retire.

Life is a gift. As you look around you see people who are so enmeshed in the details of life, settling into the routines of Monday through Friday, that they are missing the gift. Celebrate!

> Human beings were made for celebration!
> Celebrate presence!
> Celebrate God's love!
> Celebrate God's purpose!
> Celebrate God's Son!
> Celebrate the gift of relationships!
>
> > Celebrate life!

The first part of this strategy of transformation is to connect people to the rhythmic lifestyle of celebration in a language that they understand.

Chapter 5

cell

"All who believed were together."
Acts 2:44

"We don't like what we are seeing in your marriage." The words stung. Carolyn and I had been members of a Sunday night home group that had been meeting every other week for more than two years. Bill and Donna, Jeff and Mindy, and Barb and Jim had become some of our best friends. We were raising our children together, celebrating birthday and holiday events. We even made annual pilgrimages to a summer cottage on Lake Erie.

The words stung because they were coming from friends. Even more, I knew they were true. Our Christian sisters and brothers loved us enough to hold us accountable. I felt failure and shame. I am a pastor who belongs to Jesus Christ, who believes the Bible, and wants to live a life that honors God. Yet I was failing in my marriage.

Like many couples of our era, we were married in our early twenties. I still had to complete my senior year of college and three years of seminary while working as a youth minister in a Midwestern city, two hours away.

> "Carolyn, after I finish my senior year we will have
> more time for each other . . . "
> "After seminary . . . "
> "After we get the ministry rolling in our new
> church . . . "
> "After," "After," "After . . . "

But "after" never comes. The next thing you know you wake up, have been married ten years, and don't even know each other. You have been living a parallel existence, focusing on projects and neglecting the relationship that holds so much promise.

"We don't believe in divorce. We'll tough it out for Jesus."

This sounds familiar from so many counseling sessions. You end up living your life in numbness.

"We don't like what we are seeing in your marriage." A confrontation had come. You can run and you can hide in the worship celebration of your church. You can even hide behind the pulpit. But when you are committed to a small circle of intimate friends, they will find you out!

Worship celebration is for the purpose of faith and focus. Worship is a reality check: a movement from illusion to reality. But worship is not sufficient by itself to bring about lasting life change. Transformation happens in the safe spaces of caring friendships. Friends who love us unconditionally for who we are and yet hold us accountable for our promises at the same time.

> "Day by day, as they spent much time together in the
> **temple**, they broke bread at **home** and ate their food
> with glad and generous hearts, praising God and having
> the goodwill of all the people. And day by day the Lord
> added to their number those who were being saved."
>
> Acts 2:46-47

The New Testament church met in the temple, with emphasis on celebration, faith, and focus on ministry. The early church also met in the home, with emphasis on community, unconditional love, and accountability.

Created For Community

God calls us into community. We are created for community. That is why we are born into families and not institutions or classrooms. We grow in the incubation of healthy relationships. We cannot survive alone!

Community is modeled in the Trinity as the relationship between God the Father, God the Son, and God the Holy Spirit. Rugged individualism is not the model of the Kingdom of God. God created us as sexual beings, man and woman, so that we could live together as equals in community. "Therefore a man leaves his father and his mother and clings to his wife, and they become one flesh" (Genesis 2:24). Community was broken as result of the fall. Man tries to be above woman, whites over blacks, countries overpower countries, clergy over laity. A hierarchical tower of Babel was never God's intent! Jesus restores community. Look at his prayer the night before his death.

"The glory that you have given me I have given them,
so that they may be one, as we are one, I in them and
you in me, that they may become completely one, so
that the world may know that you have sent me and
have loved them as even as you have loved me."

John 17:22-23

Together again, as equals! How can you recognize the people of Jesus? "By this everyone will know that you are my disciples, if you have love for one another" (John 13:35).

We use TV cameras in worship celebrations every week, but we have made a decision not to broadcast. People follow Jesus in groups, not as rugged individualists. Television broadcast can become a substitute for community. Why go to church when you can watch it on TV? Media should enhance, not replace, community.

Post-moderns Crave Authentic Relationships

"I think people crave to have a family; you aspire to
have one, you create one in any way you can, and I
think (Gen X) can relate to dysfunctional families
because I think everyone's in a dysfunctional family. I
don't really know a functional one."[xxxvii]

Jennifer Elise Cox
played Jan Brady in "The Brady Bunch" movie

America has been called the nation of strangers. One Gallup poll reported that four in ten Americans admit to frequent feelings of "intense loneliness." Since 1970, living alone has grown more common. By 2010, more than one in four households will be single-person homes.[xxxviii] We are a transient culture. People don't live where they grow up. We change jobs and locations with much greater frequency than our parents. North Americans are longing for a sense of belonging and an experience of being connected to a cause that is greater than themselves. Post-moderns are looking for places where they can experience community.

What are the hit TV situation comedies *Friends* and *Seinfeld* about? Small groups of friends, alternative family groups who provide each other with acceptable space for mutual encouragement and testing ideas. Cell ministry will be at the heart of the life and strategy of the effective twenty-first century congregation. Education specialists need to reinvent "traditional" education models for the purpose of supporting cell-based discipleship. Persons are not looking for a classroom experience where they can get more information. Persons are longing for belonging to a small group of intimate friends.

The Life of The Body Is In The Cell

An effective trend among growing churches is to sub-divide every ministry area in the congregation into small groups. From the parking lot attendants to the ushers; the greeters to the staff-parish relations group; bowling teams to golf teams; third-grade Sunday school classes to the Fibromyalgia support cells. People are changed through the encouragement and accountability that comes through small groups of intimate friendships.

A wealth of information has been produced on small groups during the last twenty years. Here are some highlights.

Discovery #1
One size does not fit all.

Various types of small groups are necessary to meet the individual needs of believers and seekers. God is a God of diversity. Look merely at the human race. Some of us are right-brain, some are left. One size does not fit all! But you cannot get so complex that the diversity is unmanageable. The small-group ministry can be simplified in three basic models.

Discipleship Groups

Discipleship groups consist of persons who meet on a regular basis to strengthen their walk with God, encourage and care for each other, and reach out to help others. A large part of this group's focus is "learning," as part of each meeting time together has a segment for Bible study. Discipleship groups include home groups, men's, women's, teens, and children's groups.

Support Groups

Support groups are identified for persons who seek healing and restoration to wholeness. Most support groups have a common theme such as divorce recovery, health issues, or abuse situations. "Love" makes up a large portion of support groups.

Ministry Teams

Ministry teams consist of persons with a common ministry passion for service toward a particular need. The primary focus of the cell is serving. The early church called these persons "deacons." Today we call them greeters, hospitality hosts, children's tutors, video team, worship bands, cyber ministry team, resale clothing store team, furniture warehouse workers, the team that rehabilitates houses in the inner city, parking lot attendants. The list of teams is only limited by the reach of your imagination.

A person can grow in Christ-likeness, care for another and make a contribution in any group, whether it be a ministry team, discipleship, or support group.

Discovery #2
A person stays if he or she finds a cell.

Small groups are an excellent way to assimilate people into the life of the church. A person stays in the church for two basic reasons. He or she finds fulfillment through 1) significant relationships and/or 2) significant responsibilities. If new people don't find significant relationships or responsibilities they will leave through the back door of the church within a few weeks.

Mary has been attending your church for three months. Last Sunday she signed up to be a greeter. How can you maximize this ministry opportunity for Mary? You have prepared well. Every ministry area in your church has been sub-divided into cells for the purpose of nurture and assimilation. Mary will be included in a small group of friends before she hands out her first bulletin. Her ministry team will huddle together before or after the worship experience for the purpose of mutual encouragement and prayer. The cell leader is prepared to bring the group together occasionally for social events or service outreach projects. Mary's cell leader has been trained to be the primary pastor for the six greeters who serve every Saturday evening at the 5:30 worship celebration. When Mary's six-year-old son was taken to the emergency room, her small group became the hands and feet of Jesus in a critical hour of need.

Discovery #3
Churches grow larger as they act smaller.

Take a Sunday school class of twenty and sub-divide it into four groups of five. This provides the opportunity for more people to lead, share, care, and serve. The four groups grow at a greater rate than the original group of twenty persons. This is the principle of exponential growth.

Discovery #4
Small groups provide future leaders.

Small groups provide the natural training ground for leadership development. Leadership selection and development becomes the "make it or break it" factor for health and growth in every church. The harvest is plentiful, but the laborers are few! It is too tempting to prematurely place people in positions of leadership for which they are not prepared. Resist the temptation to fill slots with warm bodies because you have a great need for new leaders. It can take a long time to recover from the turmoil caused by supporting a person who is not ready for leadership. A person should be tested before he or she is placed in a position of trust.

Potential leaders are identified as they interact with others and carry out tasks within the many diverse cells. They have opportunities to identify gifts and talents as workers in the body of Christ before they are promoted to leadership. Persons who demonstrate the gifts and spiritual maturity for leadership are recognized by their peers as those who should serve in a leadership capacity. They usually become an apprentice to a cell pastor before they are given the pastoral oversight of a group.

Our church has a Staff Parish Relations cell. (This previously was a committee with a chairperson, but now it is a task cell with a cell pastor who has the primary care responsibility for the nine persons on the ministry team. The team is responsible for the oversight and accountability of the paid church staff.) Each cell member serves on the team, based on a three-year rotation.

The cell leader identifies a member of the team who has demonstrated leadership gifts and then prepares that person to become their replacement. This approach proves to be an impressive improvement over the tired, tradition of nominating warm bodies. *Every leader is a mentor to his or her replacement.*

The best cell pastors (responsible for the care of ten persons) become team pastors (who supervise five cell pastors). When team pastors have demonstrated a certain level of expertise, they are promoted to coordinating pastors (full-time staff who supervise team pastors). As coordinating pastors demonstrate ministry skills and maturity, they become regional pastors (lead team).

We have more than seventy paid staff people at Ginghamsburg Church. Over sixty have been developed internally through this system. Three of the five regional pastors at Ginghamsburg Church began as unpaid workers in a cell. Our best success with staff selection has come through home-grown talent.

The talent is linked together by an intentional structure, which is fully known to the teams:

Lead Team

The Lead Team consists of the senior pastor and four other staff people who are responsible for broad areas of ministry. The senior pastor shares vision and direction with the Lead Team. The Lead Team is then responsible for taking the vision and direction on to the coordinating pastors.

Coordinating Pastors

Coordinating Pastors are responsible for leading specific ministries within the church, such as Children's, Teens, Adult Education, Communications, and so on. These staff members interact directly with the team pastors for supervision and implementation of the vision.

Team Pastors

Team Pastors provide support and guidance to approximately five cell pastors. Their responsibilities include communicating the vision to the cell pastors, caring for the overall health of the small group, and to communicate information back to the Lead Team through their Coordinating Pastors.

Cell Pastors

Cell pastors (small group leaders) facilitate and nurture groups of people to grow together towards spiritual maturity. These powerful communities are the church at the most intimate and caring level. Cell pastors receive care and guidance directly from the team pastors.

Apprentices

Apprentices are people who have been selected by the cell pastor to be a "cell pastor in training." Each group should have an apprentice. The apprentice assists the cell pastor with the meetings while learning from the cell pastor. The ultimate goal for the apprentice is to be equipped to lead their own group in the future.

Members

Members of small groups come from all areas. Some are long-standing members of the church, some are new to the church, and others have the small group as their only connection to the church. Our desire as a church is that all people who are attendees of a weekend worship experience would also become members of a small group.

Discovery #5
Bury the Dead.

Any time you start something new you must let go of something old.

Again, a church gets larger by getting smaller. You can't do everything well. Small-group ministry is not just another program to add to your burdened program schedule. Some churches expect people to be involved in Sunday morning worship, Sunday School, come back Sunday evening, and oh yes, there are Wednesday night prayer meeting, women's meetings, men's meetings, youth meetings, children's meetings, singles' meetings, administrative meetings, mid-week Bible studies, prayer breakfasts, revivals, retreats, circles, clubs, bazaars, pot luck dinners—bring me the Alka Seltzer!—and senior citizens groups. No leader anywhere in the congregation can do everything well. When you commit yourself to something new, you must let go of something old.

Focus your energy and resources on a simple strategy: to involve persons in the transforming rhythm of Celebration, Cell, and Call. Programs are not effective change agents. Simplify and focus! See what God can do when you move out of the church building and into the homes of loving, caring friends. The central meeting place for the New Testament church was the home (Acts 2:46; 5:42).

Discovery #6
Stay flexible!

At times we have been too legalistic in our attempts to apply particular models of ministry to our local church context. Models work better on paper than they do under pressure. Over time a church becomes more flexible in the way that groups are structured. At first we will attempt to police the ratio of ten to twelve people in a group, and that each group shall have an apprentice. These are important principles but the harder we try to enforce strict rules, the less persons will participate. When we become more flexible and use the "rules" as a guide, not law, we suddenly see among leaders a great increase in enthusiasm and creativity in accomplishing the real goal of discipleship.

One home group will likely give birth to multiple new groups, but still seem to maintain a group size of around thirty. This breaks the rules according to everything we will study about cell ministry. We are now asking different questions: 1) Are the group leaders healthy? 2) Are the members of the group healthy? 3) Are persons growing into mature disciples?

Overall size of the group is not the most important element of the group. A person *can* become a disciple in many different sizes of groups. The main concern is that each person shall be connected in some way to the congregation apart from the celebration service. Significant relationships and responsibilities (connections) are more important than group size.

Post-moderns resist standardization, centralization, maximization, concentration, and bureaucratization.[xxxix] Ministry models of the twenty-first century Church will be based on unique needs and customized ideas. Many people are introduced to the Gospel of Jesus Christ in the informal space of a home or support group, who never really trust or become fully involved in the larger programs of the institutional Church. Adapt, change, try new things, risk failure. One size does not fit all!

Marriages Can Be Resurrected!

On August 26, 1997, Carolyn and I celebrated our 25th wedding anniversary. Carolyn is my best friend. I cannot believe that God has given me this incredible gift. Our relationship is more important to me than my church or ministry. How did this miracle take place after years of pain and numbness? I'm not exactly sure. But I do know that we had a small group of friends who loved us enough to hold us accountable. And they prayed through our dark hours when we forgot how.

Through the love of others Jesus still works miracles. We experience God's power and unconditional love through people who literally become to us the presence of Christ.

Chapter 6

call

"Before I formed you in the womb I knew you, and before you were born I consecrated you; I appointed you a prophet to the nations."
Jeremiah 1:5

"You did not choose me but I chose you. And I appointed you to go and bear fruit, fruit that will last."
John 15:16

Destine. "To set or appoint to a purpose; to design; to ordain."

Susan, in her mid forties, is a senior partner in a large Midwestern law firm. She grew up in a county seat, mainline church, but got out of the habit of attending when she went away to college. The campus climate of the late 60s and 70s gave Susan plenty of opportunity to invest her energy in important causes. She helped organize the first Earth Day on her campus, marched in an anti-war rally and demonstrated for civil rights. Her interest in law grew out of her desire to represent the poor. The summer between her junior and senior year afforded Susan the opportunity to work in a public defender's office. It was all the inspiration that was needed. Susan knew that she would give herself to a career that would make a difference in the lives of other persons who didn't have all of the opportunities that she grew up with.

Susan graduated near the top of her law class. Several prestigious firms courted her in the winter months of her senior year. She did have school loans to pay. "Why not get out of school, work awhile, pay off loans, and then go into advocacy work?"

Susan was married, had two children, and later divorced. The pace of success and cost of raising two children as a single parent no longer afforded her the opportunity to realize her dream. Her oldest son has now gone to college and the youngest will leave in two more years. As Susan approaches fifty she spends more time reflecting on unrealized dreams and future possibilities. The college environment allowed many opportunities for her to invest her time and energy in life-changing endeavors. Now her days seem to consist of endless meetings, conferences, and corporate mergers. She longs for the opportunity to make her life count.

Each person, no matter how disadvantaged, has an innate desire to make a difference, to know that this life matters. God has created each person with such a destiny. We know this because Jesus has come into the world to help us live out God's purpose.

> "After he had washed their feet, had put on his robe
> and had returned to the table, he said to them, 'Do you
> know what I have done to you? You call me Teacher and

Lord—and you are right, for that is what I am. So if I,
your Lord and Teacher, have washed your feet, you also
ought to wash one another's feet. For I have set you an
example, that you also should do as I have done to you.'"

John 13:12-15

Jesus calls us to do God's work just as he was sent to do the work
of "his Father." The most exciting discovery of my life has been the
realization that I am called by God to be directly involved in God's
redemptive purpose on planet Earth. Jesus liberates each of us to
fulfill our God-given destinies.

"Very truly, I tell you, the one who believes in me
will also do the works that I do and, in fact, will do
greater works than these, because I am going to the
Father."

John 14:12

When Mother Theresa died, barefoot paupers, movie stars, and
government leaders waited outside a Calcutta church in a mon-
soon rain for a chance to file by her body. She was given a state
funeral by the Indian government, which is an honor usually
reserved for heads of state. Three months before her death she
received the highest civilian honor bestowed by the United States
Congress. Why was this Nobel Peace Prize recipient held with
such high esteem and honor by people of all faiths and stations in
life? Mother Theresa understood and lived God's call. A four-foot,
nine-inch testimony that God wills great things through ordinary
people. She often referred to herself as a "pencil" in the hands of
the Lord. She began her charity work in Calcutta, India, in 1950.
Her order now has more than 4,000 nuns and runs 517 orphan-
ages, homes for the poor, AIDS hospices, and other charity centers
around the world.[xl] Mother Theresa never counted herself special
or unique. When praised for her accomplishments, "It is because
of Jesus," she said.

To discover and live out God's destiny. To be an instrument in the
hands of God. What destiny does God have for you?

Meetings or Mission?

Susan noticed one of her associates spending late hours in the library on her way out of the office building.

"Gary, why don't you go home? I appreciate your diligence, but you need some down time."

"Oh, this isn't for the firm. It is a volunteer project that I have gotten involved in with my church."

"What does a church have to do with a law library?"

"Our church has started a volunteer counseling program in a government housing project. I give two nights a month to people who can't afford legal counsel. It is really very fulfilling."

"Doesn't sound like the church that I remember. All that my mom and dad ever did was go to meetings. I don't think they ever got involved with people in need. Well, let me know if you ever need any help. Sounds like something I might have some time for. Good night. See you tomorrow."

Time is a precious commodity for post-moderns. Societal, familial, and employment changes have made churched and unchurched persons busier than ever. The average person has less than two hours a week to give to a volunteer organization. The competition for those hours is intense. Schools, service clubs, community youth organizations, local governments, and various non-profit agencies all compete for a piece of the pie. A person does not want to spend all day at work, come to a church meeting, and then sit around for several hours and argue over nothing more significant than what color to paint the fellowship hall. Churches that are successfully reaching unchurched populations are redefining themselves by eliminating most of the committee-based organizational models. Jesus didn't give his life so people could come to an administrative meeting. Move the volunteers out of meetings and into real mission. Persons are energized when they are involved in a ministry that makes a difference *and* fits their needs and gifts.

Walter is a banker who was unchurched until he came to church with his wife Shirley on a Saturday evening.

"My wife, Shirley, was the main influence on me coming to

church. She had started attending, and I was impressed with how Jesus was working in her life. She was excited to be part of the Body of Christ, and I wanted what she had. From age eighteen through my mid-fifties, I did not attend church except for an occasional visit. I started visiting on Saturday nights, and I could feel the presence of Jesus in the congregation."

Walter came to the church on the arm of a friend: his wife. But he could have very likely fallen through the cracks if he was not assimilated into the life of the church at a point beyond worship.

"Shirley was coming on Sundays to be part of a class, so I attended on Sunday to be with her. I started attending both Sunday school and a worship service, never thinking that I would dedicate my life to Jesus Christ. I was baptized and became a member."

Discipleship means service. Jesus calls us to follow in a lifestyle of giving so that others may have life. Worship and Sunday School are inadequate without the challenge and opportunity to make a difference in the lives of others.

See CD ROM: *Multi-sensory Worship, Mission Moments*

"Before coming, I volunteered in Partners In Education, a tutoring program with the local school system in my community. I was transferred to a new job location and was unable to continue the tutoring. I realized that God had been so good to me my entire life. It was time in my life to give back to God. My wife suggested that since I had worked well with children in the past and enjoyed it, I might want to work with the Clubhouse tutoring program through our church. Shirley knew someone involved in the Clubhouse ministry and that person introduced me to the director. I began working at the Old North Clubhouse in Dayton, one day per week."

In most instances, a banker would have been invited to serve on the finance committee. Walter's attendance might have exhibited absenteeism and tardiness. Why? Because a banker is a busy person, and church committee meetings tend to get lost in the hectic pace of daily routines. Besides, *church meetings are not life changing; they are boring!* Don't place volunteers in meetings. Give each person the opportunity to touch a real person's life, directly in a mission that produces "hands-on" results.

ROUTES OF ASSIMILATION

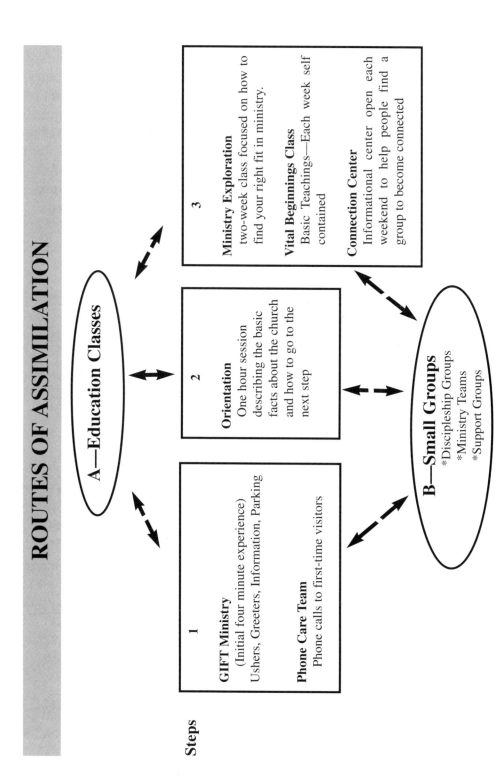

Steps

A—Education Classes

1

GIFT Ministry
(Initial four minute experience)
Ushers, Greeters, Information, Parking

Phone Care Team
Phone calls to first-time visitors

2

Orientation
One hour session describing the basic facts about the church and how to go to the next step

3

Ministry Exploration
two-week class focused on how to find your right fit in ministry.

Vital Beginnings Class
Basic Teachings—Each week self contained

Connection Center
Informational center open each weekend to help people find a group to become connected

B—Small Groups
*Discipleship Groups
*Ministry Teams
*Support Groups

"I met Daniel at the Old North Clubhouse. Daniel lives in a housing project with a single mom who is giving her best to raise four children. Daniel grew up in the Clubhouse program and was in the seventh grade. He had started attending a discipleship group, but his group leader moved out of state. The director asked if I would consider being the group leader for Daniel and two other inner-city boys. I knew nothing about discipleship groups, but I asked God for guidance and the group continued. We now have five boys in our group, all from the inner city. I thank God for the opportunity to be a part of their lives. It's challenging at times, but very rewarding."

Persons want to make a difference, to know that they are part of the solution and not the problem in the lives of other persons. Walter is a growing disciple of Jesus because someone had the good sense to ask him to serve others, and not on a committee.

Walter has gone the extra mile with Daniel and is having a real impact on Daniel's whole family. Daniel's mother, Tammy, has recently joined our staff team. Walter makes sure that Daniel has the opportunity to go on mission trips and attend church on a regular basis. He also worked with Daniel through some difficult times of rebellion, when Daniel had difficulty in school.

Persons are drawn to churches that demonstrate the power of Jesus' compassion. Three times a day, 365 days a year, members of Glide Memorial United Methodist Church, in San Francisco, work to feed hungry people. On a typical Sunday afternoon, the line of homeless hungry persons stretches for blocks. More for than 6,500 persons come on Thanksgiving. Church members sign up to help serve the dinner to the homeless and needy. On one occasion the number of volunteers was limited to 1,200. Glide has become the most comprehensive nonprofit provider of human services in San Francisco. Glide averages 2,500 people at two high energy worship services where there are no hymnals and the organ hasn't been played in years. There are over 35 programs, from drug recovery to computer training. The pastor, Cecil Williams, has been known to walk into crack houses with church members, shouting "It's recovery time!" through a megaphone. "At Glide, we believe that the true church stays on the edge of life, where the real moans and groans are," Williams says. "Most church folks settle in, get comfortable and build doctrinal walls to protect themselves from anyone who thinks or looks differently than they do."[xli] Bill Cosby, Maya Angelou, Oprah Winfrey, the late Leonard Bernstein, John F. Kennedy Jr., and the rock group U2 are just some of the people who have been seen hanging out at Glide. Some may disagree with Williams' theological claims, but his actions of compassion put many of us to shame. Jesus said that we can tell his disciples by the way they show love to one another.

Unchurched persons are not going to leave home for the safe and comfortable, the nice and happy confines of a local church. Why should they? They already have safe and comfortable. What they don't have is the sense of fulfillment that comes from making a difference. Post-moderns want to invest their time and resources in those places that are making a difference.

It is time for the church to rediscover the radical counter-culture mission of Jesus and move **out on the edge**. Jesus calls us to move beyond our contributions to commitment. Jesus didn't die for dinners, bazaars, and "country club" church meetings. Jesus died and then rose from the grave so that the captives could be set free. He calls us to follow in costly discipleship.

> "As they were going along the road, someone said to him, 'I will follow you wherever you go.' And Jesus said to him 'Foxes have holes, and birds of the air have nests; but the Son of man has nowhere to lay his head.' To another he said, 'Follow me.' But he said, 'Lord, first let me go and bury my father.' But Jesus said to him, 'Let the dead bury their own dead; but as for you, go and proclaim the kingdom of God.' Another said, 'I will follow you, Lord; but let me first say farewell to those at my home.' Jesus said to him, 'No one who puts a hand to the plow and looks back is fit for the kingdom of God.'"
>
> Luke 9:57-62

To be fully given over to the purpose of God, without condition or excuse, is life. Nothing else—not money, sex, food, success, or any other relationship can replace God's destiny.

The call of God is not only for those involved in professional ministry. God has created every human being with a divine purpose. The greatest thing we can do for another human being is to help each person discover God's call!

> "A core characteristic of the twenty-first century church is the mobilization of the laity. In 21st Century churches, there is a high value placed on mobilization with each person seen as having a gift, role and place to serve. There is a systematic approach to the process of identifying gifts and talents, equipping/coaching and placement for service and mobilization is implemented by a leadership team with a designated point person for lay mobilization."[xlii]

The church of the twenty-first century is simplifying its structure to help members focus less on "busyness" and more on God's purpose as it relates to call and an individual's gift/talent mix. In an age of frantic pace and complexity, the church will help people clarify and simplify. God creates people for Kingdom involvement, not church busyness!

How shall we downsize? Ask persons to involve themselves in the transformational rhythm of Celebration, Cell, and Call. For many, the call may not happen within the boundaries of the church campus. Most people will not "come to church" to do ministry. It is the church's job to prepare disciples to be salt and light in the world.

Questions that Help Individuals to Identify Call/Gift/Role

1. What is your passion?

2. Where do you see the greatest need?

3. What gifts/talents/strengths has God given you to meet that need?

4. What qualities or gifts do other people affirm in you? (If it doesn't energize other people, it may be an interest but is not a gift.)

5. Where do you see positive results from the investment of your involvement?
    Does it make a difference in other people's lives?
    Does it cause people to see God in a clearer way?

6. As you pursue the passion, what doors open and what doors are closed?

Part Three

How To Build Teams
That Speak Effectively
in the Culture

Introduction:
The Movement From
Stability to
Turbulence

The one word that describes the time we live and minister in is *change*. The TV remote control is a fitting metaphor for the rapid pace, constant flow of information, introduction of new ideas and products, ever-expanding networks, the easily bored and distracted, new global community. Change is the one post-modern constant that you can count on.

The environment of *continual* rapid change is a relatively new phenomenon. Just look at what's happened in the business community. From the end of World War II until 1985 there was a lengthy period of relative stability, which was reinforced by the type of hierarchy and precision that was required to plunge a world into war. Almost all change was planned and managed. You could plan future strategy from the history of past success. The motto that grew out of this stable, planned-growth era was "If it ain't broke, don't fix it!"

After 1985, turbulence became the norm, rather than the anomaly, for business operation. Steve Reinemund, CEO of Frito-Lay Corp., met with a group of pastors in Phoenix in the fall of 1992. He shared with us how Pizza Hut had gone from a highly profitable company that led in market share in 1985 to a company that was in trouble just one year later. What was the difference? Domino's had come on the scene, and Domino's delivered! It didn't matter that Pizza Hut was the number-one choice for pizza taste. North Americans preferred convenience over taste, and Domino's was winning market share. Reinemund was made CEO and Pizza Hut not only continued to focus on pizza taste but home and office delivery as well. Pizza Hut "delivery only" stores began to show up in communities. Cardboard advertisements in motel rooms greeted me at night when I would come in from a speaking engagement, too tired to seek food elsewhere. The new motto for doing business in the post-modern world: "Fix it before it breaks."

This movement from stability to turbulence has created tremendous demands for leadership. The critical question for church leadership: How do you lead in the midst of constant change and turbulence?

Chapter 7

Mindsets That Must Change

"Indeed, the body does not consist of one member
but of many . . .
If all were a single member,
where would the body be?"
1 Corinthians 12:14; 19

Mindset #1:
The Lone-Ranger Mentality

My seminary education, more than twenty years ago, assumed a relatively stable, linear, modern environment where sermon preparation and church administration would be done in the middle and later years of my ministry in the same way they were in the beginning. The weekly calendar was carefully laid out in linear segments, accounting for study, sermon preparation, administrative planning, meetings, counseling appointments, and hospital visitation. In addition to the role of resident preacher, I was the secretary, youth minister, janitor, primary purchasing agent, and mimeograph machine expert! "If it is going to be, it depends on me!" This linear, authoritarian, rugged individualist approach should be buried! It is exhausting, ineffective, and not biblical.

The possibility of shifting to a collaborative approach to leadership and worship came suddenly. Five members of our church staff were attending a Leadership Network conference together in Minneapolis, Minnesota. We saw the media reformation unfold before our eyes. Doug Murren, from East Side Four Square Church in Seattle, presented his content by using a computer with Power Point software, instead of with an overhead projector.

"This is revolutionary," I remember thinking at the time. "Just think of the possibilities." Doug's presentation was rather basic, with simple text and still pictures, but on that June afternoon in 1994 I could see the future. "What if you used video instead of stills in the presentation?" You can bring interviews, current event highlights, and movie clips right into the text of the message." The possibilities raced through my head.

My paradigm had been shifted. I had joined the media reformation and the post-literate age. We had to get there in our own church, but how? "I can't do this by myself . . . I can't even process words on a computer." (Don't tell anybody, but I am in my study at home writing this book in longhand on a legal pad.)

We cannot do post-modern ministry by ourselves. It would take me multiple lifetimes to learn just a fraction of the technology that we incorporate into our weekly worship celebrations. *It is not about learning how. It is about building self-directed teams of people who can.*

Six months after the meeting in Minneapolis we began using various types of visual and audio media in the weekend worship celebrations. One of the most significant changes in my ministry has been the shift to team ministry.

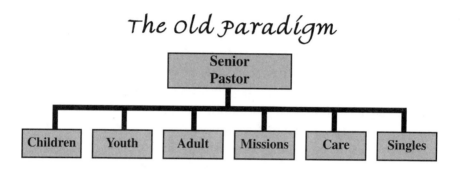

The old paradigm

From 1979 until 1994, I assembled division leaders who were "rugged individualists," who would build autonomous congregations. This model is dependent upon strong, charismatic leadership. It can create resentment and definitely fosters competition between division leaders who are aggressively pursuing the best people and resources to make their individual area a success. The youth minister was rewarded for the growth of the youth program; how many new youth cells, youth in Sunday School, number of youth on mission trips, etc. He was never asked about adult or children's ministry.

Staff meeting was one of the most painful times of the week. I couldn't understand why the staff members were not excited about being there. We would evaluate the past week's worship experience, review weekly reports in a round-table fashion, and cover budget concerns. The frequent glances at watches did not go unnoticed. *Everyone was in a hurry to get back to their own work.* "Why can't they see the big picture?" I kept asking myself.

The New Paradigm: Self-Directed Ministry Teams

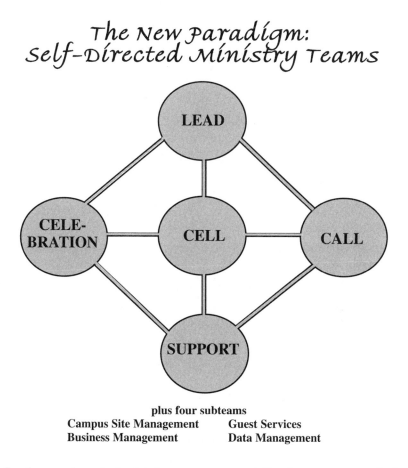

plus four subteams

Campus Site Management	Guest Services
Business Management	Data Management

In the modern industrial age, most contributions were made by entrepreneurs such as Ford, Edison, and Disney. In the post-modern world, there are no more Thomas Edisons. Great contributions are made through the collaborative efforts of teams. Teams are more effective and durable in the navigation of turbulent times. Ongoing collaborative relationships stimulate creativity and consistent exceptional performance.

Dreamworks is the first major motion picture studio to be formed in the last half of the twentieth century. Steven Spielberg, David Geffen, and Jeffrey Katzenberg have teamed their expertise and resources to do movie making in a new way. Past competitors have joined in cooperation. In the same way, the old hierarchical model of pastor as CEO giving close supervision to a group of subordinates (or volunteers) is giving way to the non-authoritarian, design of team, which also happens to be consistent with a New Testament understanding of church membership.

> "But God has so arranged the body, giving the greater honor to the inferior member, that there may be no dissension within the body, but the members may have the same care for one another. If one member suffers, all suffer together with it; if one member is honored, all rejoice together with it."
>
> 1 Corinthians 12:24-26

The book *Empowered Teams* identifies key distinguishing characteristics of self-directed teams:
- They are empowered to share various management and leadership functions.
- They plan, control, and improve their own work processes.
- They set their own goals and inspect their own work.
- They often create their own schedules and review their performance as a group.
- They may prepare their own budgets and coordinate their work with other departments.
- They usually order materials, keep inventories, and deal with suppliers.
- They are frequently responsible for acquiring any new training they might need.
- They may hire their own replacements or assume responsibility for disciplining their own members.
- They—not others outside the team—take responsibility for the quality of their products or services.[xliii]

Not everyone is a team player. The success of the team is directly related to whom you recruit to the team. Whenever possible, recruit staff from within. All paid and unpaid staff positions in your church should be filled only by people who are deeply committed to the core values and vision of your church and add to the bottom line of your mission. They are persons who understand and are deeply committed to the core vision and values. At the heart of every great team is a shared dream! These persons have also demonstrated ministry skill at multiple levels within your church that other leaders have had an opportunity to observe. The environmental learning curve, which is adjustment to a new culture, is almost nonexistent.

Do potential staff members fit in both halves of the circle?

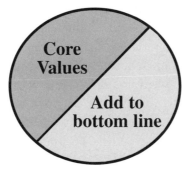

Mindset #2: Clearly Defined Job Descriptions

Flexibility! Flexibility! Flexibility! Next to character, flexibility is one of the most important traits in team ministry. Clearly defined job descriptions can function like a straight-jacket in a climate of change. "That's not in my job description!" These six words destroy the spirit of team. Teammates should be able to play wherever they are needed.

We didn't have a multi-media expert on staff when we started using media in worship. Our missions pastor had a broad knowledge of computers, knew how to work a VCR, and was willing to learn a software presentation package. Mike jumped into the media booth for the first six months until we could find someone who was trained in media. By the time he came out of the media booth, we needed his prior business expertise in our accounting office. Mike was hired to organize our missions teams, but he spent at least half of his time working in media or finance. When flexibility is the key in team ministry, service is based on gifts and need—not on job description.

Mindset #3: Long-Range Planning

"You should have a sermon file and plan your sermons at least one year in advance." How many of us were given this directive in our training for ministry? I often felt guilty come Wednesday afternoon when I cried out, "O God, help! Give me a word for this weekend!"

This is the mindset that people bring when they ask, "How long does it take to plan and prepare your worship experience?" From the specially produced video segments, drama, thematic music pieces to the media-enriched message, most people figure that each week takes at least a month to develop. They have trouble believing that the whole process begins on Wednesday morning with just a seed idea and then is ready to go in its entirety by Saturday afternoon (see Chapter 4: Celebration).

Time Magazine does not know what is going to be on the cover in two weeks. *USA Today* does not know what the headline will be two days from now. High powered, self-directed editorial teams can not afford the luxury of long-range planning in a medium that exists for the purpose of communicating current significant events in a bottom-line fashion to a culture that suffers from information overload. The competition for people's attention is intense! These teams must be ready to change and make adjustments at a moment's notice, day in and day out.

When Princess Diana died in a tragic car accident, news teams were ready to go on air in a matter of minutes, and the timing was midnight on the weekend! All major news anchors were doing live broadcasts from London by Sunday afternoon; ready to adapt and respond at a moment's notice.

It took many months for the Watergate scandal to unfold in 1973 and 1974. The investigation of the President in 1998 took a week or two to unfold on 24 hour cable and Internet news services.

I am not advocating the absence of long-range planning. The news networks are prepared to respond to breaking news quickly because they have planned and built structures for rapid response.

This kind of rapid response is familiar to us on the mission field which is often defined by disaster relief. My denomination is usually the first to supply physical aid to disaster victims, even before humanitarian agencies arrive. The local church must build team structures that allow for quick response to people's felt needs. We must commit ourselves to a "day by day" perspective—and not merely year to year. The Japanese call such responsiveness *kaizen*, in the context of business change. *Kaizen* refers to "constant change" for the purpose of continuous improvement.

Mindset #4: Seminary Trained

Seminary-trained leaders are at times the least prepared to speak the language of a post-Christian, post-literate, post-modern culture. Kim Miller is the Creative Arts and Worship Coordinator at Ginghamsburg. She develops all of the written prayers and "connecting" pieces for the different elements of the worship celebration. Those of us who are seminary-trained depend upon her input, editing, and rewriting, because our language tends to be too "churchy" and out of touch.

"Oh Lord, we laud and magnify thy most Holy name . . ." Well, you get the point. Kim doesn't have a bachelor's degree. Vocationally a seamstress, she has experience and passion in theater. Kim is the norm rather than the exception for the congregation of the twenty-first century.

Len Wilson is a seminary graduate. Len specialized in communications as both an undergraduate and graduate student before attending seminary. He interned at CBS. Len never pursued ordination. He specializes in media ministry on Ginghamsburg's staff. Len is the norm rather than the exception for the twenty-first century congregation.

Mindset #5: A Committee or Staff Group is the Same as a Team

The church is often quick to adopt new buzzwords without really changing behaviors or attitudes. "*Team* is the hot new concept. We will no longer call our committees, *committees*. Our committees are now teams." This is an innocuous pronouncement that does not threaten the time-honored practice of "doing business as usual." *A committee does not a team make.* Committees tend to have a purpose that does not participate in results.

I am a member of the Board of Trustees of one of our denominational seminaries. We meet three times a year for the specific purpose of *evaluating* the progress and status of the seminary and *approving* major actions. This is the typical purpose of a church committee or staff group that meets together once a week or month: *evaluate, approve, and delegate.* A team, on the other hand, *dreams, develops* and *deploys* the necessary action steps for accomplishment together. It is more than the organization of individual pieces. The team travels together through the entire journey. The team also *evaluates* and "owns" its own results.

Under our fatigued model, worship was designed by several certified, expert individuals. The minister of music (lay or professional) would work with the choir, solo special(s), and worship outline. Or the "praise team" leader would choose songs for congregational singing, and then work with the band. The pastor would work on the sermon. Each of the pieces would be brought together, and sometimes discussed in advance, for the weekend worship experience.

Team is more than the organization of the individual parts. The team dreams, develops, and deploys the entire process together. Each team member has a part in the sermon as well as the music. Our Celebration team travels the worship journey together from Wednesday through Sunday.

Enough with the words. It's time to *experience* the rhythm, linkages, and vibrations of what this book can do to change your worship into a Celebration.

Chapter 8

Multi-Sensory Worship

This edition of *Out on the Edge* is packaged with the CD-ROM, *Multi-sensory Worship*. The CD-ROM is set up in four interactive modules, including:

Imagining: a process is offered for transforming the worship design team into a media-savvy ministry that can speak the language of the people. The team members (described on page 77) offer practical advice about the weekly preparation for celebration. Quicktime movies illustrate the process.

Linking: Six typical worship scenarios are included, to demonstrate the graphical and audio content of post-reformation Celebrations. Each scenario represents one of the basic felt needs, as described on page 79.

Experiencing: A video portfolio of mission moments, calls to worship, and testimonials are presented through Quicktime movies. Each celebration is a communication event, and this portfolio includes samples from communication campaigns that envelope the event.

Browsing: If you need to search for an idea or suggestion, this module contains the text of the book, *Out on the Edge*.

How to view Multi-sensory Worship

QuarkImmedia Viewer is a stand-alone application that allows anyone to view and interact with QuarkImmedia projects. The QuarkImmedia Viewer is distributed royalty-free.

QuarkImmedia Viewer 1.04 is available for Windows, Macintosh, and Power Macintosh. The Windows version is compatible with Windows 3.1, Windows for Workgroups 3.11, and Windows 95.

You can download the latest version from www.quark.com, but we have included a copy of version 1.05 on the CD-ROM, which will be installed to your hard-drive. *Multi-sensory Worship*, however, is hundreds of megabytes, containing many movies, and will be run from your CD-ROM player. You will need a sound card with speakers to fully appreciate the sounds and the graphics. Minimum requirements are a 486 processor and 8MB of RAM with 256 colors for the monitor. We have obtained best viewing results with at least a Pentium 133 mghz, 32MB of RAM, and at least an 8x CD-ROM.

Windows installation:
To install QuarkImmedia Viewer on your hard-drive, from the Program Manager (Windows 3.1) or the Start Menu (Windows 95), select RUN, X:\install.exe, where X is the letter of your CD-ROM drive. Close all open applications and follow the screen directions. When the viewer is installed, launch it from the program group or desktop. You may open *Multi-sensory Worship*, by selecting FILE\Open X\worship.imd. See the file Read_1st.wri for further information.

Macintosh installation:
Copy the Quarkimmedia Viewer file to the hard drive of your computer. (You can run Quarkimmedia Viewer directly from the CD, but performance may improve if you run it from your hard drive.) Double click the file Worship on the CD to play *Multi-sensory Worship*.

Notes

"Church Just Doesn't Make Sense"

i   Thomas C. Reeves, *The Empty Church* (New York: Free Press, 1996), p. 62.

ii   *Ibid.*, p. 63.

iii   International Centre for Leadership Development, Canada.

iv   *Newscope: A Newsletter for United Methodist Church Leaders,* Volume 25, Number 28 (July 11, 1997), p. 3.

Introduction:
The Electronic Media Pentecost

v   *Leadership Journal,* "Pastoring with Integrity in a Market-Driven Age," Kent Hughes, Brian Larson, Lyle Schaller (Summer 1997), p.114.

vi   Statistic given by Len Wilson, Minister of Media at Ginghamsburg Church, in a presentation to the Texas Conference of the United Methodist Church, Houston (February 1997).

vii   Tim Celek and Dieter Zander, Inside the Soul of a New Generation (Grand Rapids: Zondervan Publishing House, 1996), p. 63.

viii   *Ibid.*, p.62.

ix   Michele Galen and Karen West, "Companies Hit the Road Less Traveled: Can Spirituality Enlighten the Bottom Line?" *Business Week* (June 5, 1995), p. 82.

x   Robert G. Duffett, *A Relevant Word* (Valley Forge: Judson Press, 1995), p.77.

A Post-literate Age

xi   Leslie Newbigin, *Foolishness To The Greeks* (Grand Rapids: Wm. B. Eerdmans Publishing Company, 1986), p. 25.

xii   Howard Snyder, *The Problem Of Wineskins* (Downers Grove: Inter-Varsity Press, 1975), p. 33.

xiii   Kenneth Miller, "Star Struck," *Life Magazine* (July 1997), p. 39.

xiv   Michele Galen and Karen West, "Companies Hit The Road Less Traveled: Can Spirituality Enlighten The Bottom Line?" *Business Week* (June 5, 1995), p. 82.

xv   Tony Mauro, "Justice Scalia says religion, reason do mix," *USA Today* (April 10, 1996).

xvi   Robert W. Burtuer and Robert Chiles, *A Compendia of Wesley's Theology* (Nashville: Abingdon Press, 1954), p. 20.

xvii   Lyle E. Schaller, *The New Reformation: Tomorrow Arrived Yesterday* (Nashville: Abingdon Press, 1995), p. 107.

The Word Became Flesh

xviii   The dove is used in Scripture as a sign of God's approval or providential involvement. The dove retured to Noah, "and there in its beak was a freshly plucked olive leafe; so Noah knew that the waters had subsided from the earth" (Genesis 8:11). Dove and Spirit are associated together at Jesus' baptism. "And when Jesus had been baptized, just as he came up from the water, suddenly the heavens were opened to him and he saw the Spirit of God descending like a dove and alighting on him" (Matthew 3:16).

xix   The story of the woman of Samaria (John 4).

Wineskins Change!

xx   Matthew 9:17.

xxi   The construction of the Tabernacle (Exodus 35).

xxii   Howard A. Snyder, *The Problem of Wineskins* (Downers Grove, IL, Inter-Varsity Press, 1975), p. 15-16.

xxiii   James C. Collins and Jerry Porras, *Built to Last: Successful Habits of Visionary Companies* (New York, NY: Harper Collins, 1994, 1997), p. 66.

xxiv   Tex Sample, *Ministry In An Oral Culture* (Louisville, Westminster/John Knox Press, 1994), p. 3.

xxv   Edited by Bernard McGinn, John Mayendorff, and Jean Leclerq,

Christian Spirituality: Origins to the Twelfth Century (New York: Crossroads, 1989), p. 3.

xxvi   Earle Cairns, *Christianity Through The Centuries* (Grand Rapids, Zondervan Publishing House, 1954), p. 128.

xxvii   Pierre Babin, *The New Era in Religious Communication* (Minneapolis, Fortress Press, 1991), p. 18.

A Post-modern Strategy for the Third Millennium Church

xxviii Andrew Lack, news president, *NBC*.

xxix   *Ibid.*

Celebration

xxx   *Leadership, A Practical Journal for Church Leaders* (Winter 1997), "The Church's Ten Year Window—A Conversation with Futurist Faith Popcorn," p. 23-24.

xxxi   Robert G. Duffett, *A Relevant Word: Communicating the Gospel to Seekers* (Valley Forge, Judson Press, 1995), p. 79.

xxxii   Leonard Sweet, *Faithquakes* (Nashville, Abingdon Press, 1994), p. 110.

xxxiii Thomas Troeger, *Ten Strategies for Preaching in a Multi Media Culture* (Nashville, Abingdon Press, 1996), p. 12.

xxxiv   *Ibid.*, p.13.

xxxv   Lyle Schaller, *The New Reformation: Tomorrow Arrived Yesterday* (Nashville, Abingdon Press, 1995), p. 34.

xxxvi   Robert G. Duffet, *A Relevant Word: Communicating the Gospel to Seekers* (Valley Forge, Judson Press, 1995), p. 73.

Cell

xxxvii Rob Owen, *Electronic Times Union* (http://www.timesunion.com) July 17, 1997, p.3.

xxxviii *Newsweek*, (June 23, 1997), p. 23.

xxxix   Alvin and Heidi Toffler, *Creating A New Civility: The Politics of the Third Wave* (Turner Publishing, 1995).

call

xl   *USA Today* (Monday, September 8, 1997), p. 17A.

xli   *USA Today* (Wednesday, November 22, 1995) "Cover Story: Liberal Cleric's Work Attracts Critics," p. 1A.

xlii   *Net Fax: Leadership Network*, "Helping Church Leaders Make the Tr
(I

xliii   R   *ow-*
e
C
J

See p
instr